PRAISE FOR
REBEL LEADERSHIP

"LUIS URDANETA is a visionary living a life of determination, passion, and BELIEF. In this book, you will find inspiration and breakthroughs from an amazing trailblazer. A businessman with focus and great grit to manifest success in service. *Rebel Leadership* will definitely make you a better leader and human."

—ISMAEL CALA
Life Holistic Strategist
Bestselling Author
and International Speaker

"LUIS URDANETA takes readers on a journey through hardships, turmoil, and self-reflection. Read this book and you will be inspired to forge your own path and never to give up even when your situation seems unfixable."

—MARK COLE
President and CEO
Maxwell Leadership

"... AN AMAZING GUIDE for those hungry for success and looking for a way to channel their rogue energy. If you want a cookie-cutter story about success, then this book is not for you. Learn from this leader's journey to fuel your own fire."

—DON YAEGER
11-time *New York Times*
Bestselling Author

"STRUGGLE IS THE BIRTHPLACE of success. There is no achievement without adversity. Everything can be improved, and nothing is for certain. *Rebel Leadership* is the playbook for amplifying your vision and accelerating your victories. Read it and it will transform your business and your life!"

—TODD DUNCAN
New York Times Bestselling Author of
*High Trust Selling: Make More Money
in Less Time with Less Stress*

"WITH THIS BOOK you will learn lessons from 100 percent real stories and anecdotes from someone who with hustle and determination changed his whole world, the world of so many people around him, and around the world in the process."

—RAY URDANETA
CEO and Cofounder, MONAT GLOBAL

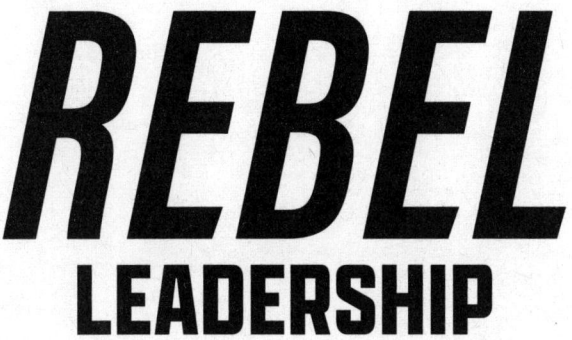

LUIS URDANETA

FOREWORD BY JOHN C. MAXWELL

REBEL
LEADERSHIP

WHY IT PAYS TO BREAK THE RULES
TO BE SUCCESSFUL IN BUSINESS AND IN LIFE

REBEL LEADERSHIP
WHY IT PAYS TO BREAK THE RULES
TO BE SUCCESSFUL IN BUSINESS AND IN LIFE

Copyright © 2023 by Luis Urdaneta

All rights reserved. No part of this publication may be reproduced, stored in a retrieval system, or transmitted in any form by any means, electronic, mechanical, photocopy, recording, or otherwise, without the prior permission of the publisher, except as provided by USA copyright law.

No patent liability is assumed with respect to the use of the information contained herein. Although every precaution has been taken in the preparation of this book, the publisher and author assume no responsibility for errors or omissions. Neither is any liability assumed for damages resulting from the use of the information contained herein.

Published by Forefront Books.
Distributed by Simon & Schuster.

Library of Congress Control Number: 2022919431

Print ISBN: 979-8-88710-012-8
E-book ISBN: 979-8-88710-013-5
Proprietary ISBN: 979-8-88710-030-2

Cover Design by George Stevens, G Sharp Design LLC
Interior Design by Mary Susan Oleson, Blu Design Concepts

TO MY LOVING AND INCREDIBLE FAMILY: my wife, Leudin, my sons, Ray and Javi, and my daughters, Lu, Luisana, and Nicole. Rebellion is a simple choice when it brings me closer to each one of you and our dreams. Thank you for being my WHY and my partners in everything I do.

TO MY PARENTS: You made me who I am. Thanks to the kindness of my dad and the discipline of my mom, I found my own formula to happiness and success.

TO MY FRIENDS AND BUSINESS PARTNERS: Thank you for helping me achieve and write a great life story.

I love you all deeply and forever.

CONTENTS

FOREWORD BY JOHN C. MAXWELL — 13

CHAPTER 1: Broken — 17

CHAPTER 2: Dreaming in Venezuela — 31

CHAPTER 3: Chasing Opportunities — 45

CHAPTER 4: Two Pink Bags — 57

CHAPTER 5: Passion and Discipline: Becoming #1 — 77

CHAPTER 6: Hitting Rock Bottom — 99

CHAPTER 7: Starting from Zero — 113

CHAPTER 8: Knowing Your Worth — 129

CHAPTER 9: Returning to Success — 147

CHAPTER 10: My Country in Ruins — 161

CHAPTER 11: For My People — 115

CHAPTER 12: Project USA — 193

CHAPTER 13: The American Dream — 209

CHAPTER 14: The Power of Empowerment — 229

CHAPTER 15: Never Lose Your Hunger — 241

CHAPTER 16: Living a Legacy — 255

CHAPTER 17: Better Never Stops — 269

ACKNOWLEDGMENTS — 283

NOTES — 287

FOREWORD
BY JOHN C. MAXWELL

ONE OF MY GREATEST passions in life is learning from other leaders. I love listening to each unique story and finding lessons to apply to my own leadership. Everyone has something to teach me. And I've found that when you ask the right questions, you will learn that every leader has a "why" that provides the fuel—the motivation—to lead.

I think Luis Urdaneta is one of the most unique leaders I've ever learned from. He has a style all his own. One of the things I love most about Luis is how he protects against "dream thieves," a nickname he has given to those who rob your aspirations, potential, and pursuits. That's a great example of how Luis values people and wants to help them succeed.

Rebel Leadership is an approach and methodology that has been proven through the various companies

FOREWORD

Luis has created as well as the success he has built from many difficult circumstances. Luis teaches that in order to be a leader, you must hold true to your values and make others successful on your way to the top because the only way to get better and go higher is by helping others. This is foundational for good leadership. It reminds me of something I heard Zig Ziglar say many years ago, "You can get everything in life you want if you will just help enough people get what they want."

Meeting Luis and working with him has been a wonderful experience. He truly is a "rebel leader" who makes everyone around him dream bigger. Luis does not speak or understand English, and still he found a way not only to be successful in the US, but globally as well. He created and launched MONAT Global, a beauty company that's now a multinational and nearly billion-dollar brand known for offering beauty products that are naturally based.

I've seen MONAT since its beginning, and I remember thinking the company and team were very special. I've always had a lot of respect for the network marketing industry, not only because it's the industry where most self-made millionaires have been born, but also because it's all about personal development, and my favorite subject: leadership.

When people share with me that they want to write

FOREWORD

a book, my first question is "Why?" I asked Luis this same question when he told us he wanted to put his story in a book. Without hesitation, he told me his goal is to inspire more people and teach them how to overcome the limitations they've placed on themselves. I knew immediately that this was a project I wanted to get behind and help in whatever way I could. I believe in this book because I've seen what Luis is capable of. The lessons he has learned through his experiences that made him successful will help you succeed too.

Luis has given us a window into his life with this book. Inside you will find his lessons, his secrets, and his heart like it has never been shared before. There is much to learn from Luis as he tells his story of a challenging childhood, the values his parents taught, and how he grew up always being the rebel in the family.

I believe this book will touch the lives of many people who are ready to test the boundaries and create success of their own. I'm hopeful that this book will bring Luis's dream to reality—to invite thousands of people around the world to dare to dream bigger.

CHAPTER 1

BROKEN

TEARS ROLLED down my cheeks as I looked out from the large living room window of our fourth-floor apartment at the streets of Maracaibo, the second-largest city in Venezuela and the capital of Zulia State. It was here, in the city nicknamed La Tierra del Sol Amada, or "The Beloved Land of the Sun," where I had built a life of dreams. As I looked across the beautiful landscape filled with towering buildings, the hot Venezuelan sun had been exchanged for a proverbial cloud.

It was by the grace of God and with hard work and focus that I reached the heights I did in Venezuela. Growing up with few resources in a depressed, poor area of the country, there was nothing pointing to a life of success. My father was a teacher and my mother was a homemaker. I was one of seven children. Since I was a child, I've said that I believed in magic because raising seven children and maintaining a family of nine on a single salary was either an act of magic or an act of God.

REBEL LEADERSHIP

I didn't take a typical path, nor did success come in a straight line, but by the time I was twenty-three years old, I had everything I could have ever wanted. I was a millionaire. In my twenties, I had reached the pinnacle of direct sales and was ranked among the top Tupperware® distributors in Venezuela. By the time I was thirty years old, I had retired. Then life started to happen. Fast-forward nearly ten years, and I was staring out the window in the city I had grown up in and built my life in, having hit rock bottom. I achieved a lot of goals by the age of twenty, but due to my mistakes, I was ruined by thirty-nine. I was broke *and* broken.

My wife, Leudin, already knew my situation because by that time we were living it day after day. My gambling addiction had grown so dire that we lost everything. I didn't stop gambling; I just didn't have any money to keep placing bets and chase my losses in hopes of a big win. For a while, friends would lend me money. Eventually, that stopped too. We were bankrupt. We didn't have money to eat, to pay rent — to do *anything*. We barely had enough money to feed our newborn baby. Those moments scar your memory.

The owners of the nine-story apartment complex lived across the hall, and we were already several months behind on rent. The wife would knock on our door to collect rent, and Leudin and I would be quiet,

BROKEN

acting as if we weren't home. Each time we left the apartment, we would open the door and check to make sure that the owners weren't home. The way the building was set up, residents would take the elevator to their floor, each of which had only two apartments, so it was always stressful wondering if we would run into the owners on our way in or out. We were filled with embarrassment. It was then that I was forced to surrender to what was going on in my life and take accountability for the wrong decisions I had made and the path to which I had diverged. There was no more money left and there were no friends whom I could count on. All I had were Leudin and my children — nothing else. I knew I had to start making hard decisions because, truthfully, there was nothing else to do except start walking a different path. That was an important realization. Sometimes we sit and we start thinking about our situations in a careful and aware way, in the right moment, before it's too late. In my case, it was forced. I was *forced* to think this way. I've always been stubborn and persistent, and through all my struggles, I told myself, *This is going to change; I'll do it. I'm going to be able to change things.* But the moment came when I had to surrender. I knew that I had to start making real changes. I had to have the guts to confront what led me astray.

I'll never forget that moment when I turned away

from the window toward Leudin. She was twenty-four to my thirty-nine, and people had always said that Leudin had married me because I had a lot of money. I had given Leudin a lot of jewelry and now she offered to give it back. "You can sell them," she told me. "You can put them in the pawn shop to help us get out of this situation." I was humiliated. Having had abundance for so many years and now having to take those gifts back was the lowest moment of my life. But the circumstances didn't allow me to dwell on it or to sulk. Our newborn baby lay asleep in her crib in the next room. It was either that or not survive — there was nothing else. I went to a nearby pawn shop with the jewelry I had given Leudin and left it all there. I left my pride there as well. We never saw the jewelry again.

In many cases when people surrender, they allow failure to defeat them. They get stuck. Many people close up and they don't start searching for alternatives to rise from rock bottom and thrive. They lose hope, they lose faith, and they lose the spirit and the willingness to go forward. Starting from scratch can be challenging, but it can also be an opportunity to do things differently. I am not a superman who has superpowers to overcome difficulties; I am simply a humble man who believes in his ideals and does not allow anyone to steal his dreams. Your passion and hunger must be stronger than everything.

BROKEN

You don't have to hit the same rock bottom that I did to begin the process of reinvention. There is a famous Chinese proverb that says, "A journey of a thousand miles begins with a single step." Maybe you're stuck in a job that you hate and you don't know where to go next. Maybe you have an addiction and you're not sure where to turn. Maybe you have depression, and you don't know how to stop crying. Are you ready to discover your next step?

The point is, we're human. You fail, you see your failure, and then you identify the cause of failure. If you fail and you don't identify your failure, you will never get out of the rut. Failures are part of the process that we are permanently living. Something I learned from direct sales is the importance of educating your mind. You have to prepare for how you will behave when you have success and for when you don't, and you need to be convinced that you can get past situations even when they are difficult.

When you accept your realities and your failures, you learn from them, you think, and you reflect on them in a positive way. But when you feel that the problem isn't you, but rather the people around you, the path doesn't open up.

You'll hear me talk about behaviors a lot. These are the things you should do in order to get to your destination — for example, having discipline, kindness, fairness, a focus on family and others, honesty, and other behaviors.

I realized that this problem I was living in was mine; it was a result of my mistakes and my actions. It was a result of many wrong decisions I'd made, and I knew that if I was able to change, I would be able to achieve the results I had achieved in the past. The path I had to walk now was going to be difficult, but I knew if I could do what I had done in the past, I could again be successful. There's a big difference between the person who is dreaming and believes it and the person who dreams it and doesn't believe it. There's a dream with an action and the proper follow-through and there's a dream with action but without that follow-through. I've lived them both. Changing your life is a matter of dreaming, believing in your dream, and acting with the conviction that you will make it with the appropriate conduct.

When I pawned Leudin's jewelry and was forced to start over, I was not defeated. As I cried in the apartment, I made Leudin a promise. "I'm going to be successful and have money again," I told her.

AMOR Y CONTROL

One of the biggest mistakes of my life was leaving behind my passion for direct selling and thinking that without it — with money and with luck — I could take on anything and be successful.

BROKEN

When I retired from direct sales in 1995 and built and opened a restaurant and gambling room, it wasn't a total mistake. Every day we make decisions that impact our lives — some more than others. We reach a fork in the road and must decide which way to go. Every decision involves risk, and risk isn't a bad thing! In fact, I believe that to find opportunities in life, people need to take risks. During my career, I've found it preferable to find the people who are willing to take the risk because those are the people who are most able to achieve their goals. But living fearlessly and taking risks is only one part of the equation. They must be followed by *actions and focus*. Retiring from direct sales and opening a restaurant and gambling room was not a mistake. It's just that I lost my focus. I went down the wrong path and lost my way. I was unfaithful, addicted to gambling, mismanaged money, and forgot about what mattered most. The risk was appropriate. The problem was my conduct. Living a fearless life can be good or bad. You have to take risks with instinct. I lost my focus, and my life came crashing down with it.

"What happened to your father?'" people in Maracaibo would ask my children. "He looks bad. His shirt is sticking out, his hair is messed up, and he doesn't look good." By the time I went bankrupt at the end of 1999, my oldest son, Ray, and his then-girlfriend, Carolina, were off to Miami in pursuit of the American Dream. We didn't even have enough money to put gas in the car. I couldn't give them even one dollar. I looked at myself in the and thought, *I am a disaster.*

What hurt the most was the image I felt I was projecting to my children after I'd been a successful entrepreneur. When Ray and Carolina moved to the United States at nineteen, they lived in a house with cousins and slept on an inflatable mattress tucked away underneath the staircase because they didn't have their own room to live in. Ray worked at Sears selling appliances and Carolina worked at McDonald's serving burgers. I couldn't do anything to help them.

That pain and disappointment inspired me to search for strength to overcome my situation. My life was crumbling and I was vulnerable. But I've always said, "Close that door, cry in your home, let it all out, then go out and face the situation you have to face with bravery and courage." I cried a lot. On Sundays, I would listen to "Amor y Control" ("Love and Control") by Rubén Blades, and every time I did, it reminded me of my children.

> *Only those with kids understand*
> *that a parent's responsibility never ends,*
> *that fathers and mothers*
> *never tire of giving their love,*

BROKEN

*that we want for you that which
we never had, that despite the problems
family is family, and affection is affection*

*How much control and how much love
should there be in the home?
A lot of control and a lot of love
to deal with the disgrace...*

I cried and cried listening to that song. I would compare it to my own failure, and the absence of two of my children 1,600 miles across international waters hit me hard. Even now I get goosebumps when I hear that song. At that moment I was frustrated, but more than feeling frustrated, I felt inspired. I told myself that I had to change. I would clean my image and transform from being a failure due to poor decisions, and I was sure that someday soon I would feel proud showing my family a better version of me. I started seeing my situation differently, and that helped me every day to find the strength and energy I needed to help my children.

Failure is a circumstance that happens to people who have courage. Many times when people fail, they stay there, but you have to learn how to manage failure, be brave, and look ahead in your life. Don't give up, even if you're in your worst situation. What came out of my life and my experience was the lesson to search for something or for someone who inspires you in difficult moments. For me it was family. Nothing else was important except for family. What became clear then and is a critical lesson today is that you need to have a reason why. That "why" is your inspiration to overcome any failure. When you have a very powerful "why," you're always going to be able to overcome obstacles, failures, and adversities. I still feel inspired today because I feel that I can still improve my image that at one point was so uncomfortable for me, my children, my family, and my friends.

There always has to be a "why," and then another "why," and many "whys" in your life. What makes you get up in the morning? What is it that you think about when you fall asleep at night? These questions help reveal the "whys" in our lives; they give us purpose. If your "whys" die, your hunger dies. If your hunger dies, your passion dies. If your passion dies, your focus dies. If your focus dies, everything is dead.

FINDING YOUR TRUE NORTH

Staring out toward Maracaibo, I knew I had no other option. "I have to go back to direct sales," I said as I wiped the tears from my face and turned around toward Leudin.

BROKEN

"I don't know anything else other than direct sales."

At that moment, when nobody would give me a chance, when my pockets were empty and I didn't have anything — it was only me and Leudin — we sat in the living room and talked about what we were going to do. "I need to find a way to survive," I told her. When you're not focused on where you want to go, it's easy to confuse your decisions. In my life, it has worked for me that whenever I focused on looking at my True North and what I wanted, no obstacles could weaken me. For so long, my True North was my family and direct sales. When I lost my focus, I lost my way. That's an important lesson: have a dream, know your dream, keep it as a True North, and when things are bad, go back to your True North and follow it. That's what I knew I had to do. Out of that moment was born a new plan we were going to take into action to change our situation and thrive. I took Leudin's jewelry to the pawn shop and started knocking on doors again.

We were starting all over again. That's an issue for a lot of people who fall. I was thirty-nine years old, and I remember asking myself, *Do I have a chance? Do I have the opportunity to achieve everything that I've done in the past at my age?* Seeing myself at the bottom and thinking about rebuilding everything, it felt almost impossible at my age. All those questions and negative thoughts dominated my mind, but at the end of the day, I didn't have a choice of doing anything else. I just had to start from zero. It doesn't matter if you've been to the peak of the mountain and stumbled or are just beginning your first climb toward the peak; at any age you can achieve your opportunities. "This is a matter of time," I told Leudin. "We're in the middle of a very difficult situation, but I know what I have to do, and together we will do it."

What I needed in that moment was courage — a lot of courage. I don't know a single person who is successful who hasn't failed. It's not that I don't know such a person, it's that such a person doesn't exist. If you start with that principle, it makes it a lot easier to digest failure when it comes. There are people in this world who say, "I don't dare to do it because I don't want to fail." Those people are already putting limitations on themselves, and those limitations create barriers on the ability to have courage in their actions. When you're afraid of failure, you're afraid of taking action. In critical moments, it's important to have courage, to have your feet on solid ground, and to make firm decisions. The one who is a coward is the one who stops trying. The cowardly one is not likely to have the inspiration needed. The cowardly one lets themselves be absorbed by difficult situations.

On the other hand, the people who are bold and

BROKEN

courageous search for the way to be inspired. In my case, I was inspired by my children, my wife, my parents, and the people who said I couldn't do it — the ones who didn't believe in me, the ones who said I was a failure, that I was irresponsible, that I was vicious, and that I was not going to be able to take that baggage off myself. There were many people around me who didn't believe in me. They didn't believe that I was going to be able to overcome my situation, and who inspired me. I converted the negative into a positive. The ones who wanted to bring me down with their negativity were my inspiration. The ones who didn't believe in me, instead of destroying me, inspired me even more.

One of the most important lessons I learned was seeing until what point you're able to trust in yourself, until what point your dreams don't die when the situation becomes difficult, and until what point you can understand that the processes in life for you to be able to accomplish your best opportunity go hand in hand with failure. How courageous and bold can you be to understand this, process it, and use it in your circumstances?

When I went knocking on the doors to return to direct sales, nobody opened them. Nobody wanted to look at me. I learned that when you have money, you have a lot of friends. And when you run out of money, the friends disappear. Nobody wanted to support me. Only a decade earlier I had been at the top in Tupperware sales. Now they saw me as a gambler. They told me I was obsolete. I lost everything for making bad decisions, for abandoning my passions, for straying from my True North. It is difficult to understand that one day you can be surrounded by a million people who claim to be more than friends, even brothers, and the next day you can be alone. Those who flatter you today will criticize you, despise you, and walk away from you as if they never knew you.

CHAPTER 2

DREAMING IN VENEZUELA

IN A SMALL, rural village some forty miles northwest of Maracaibo named Las Cuatro Bocas, Spanish for "the four mouths," my brothers and I would often walk into the nearby woods. With nothing to eat at home, we searched for *patilla*, also known as watermelon, or any other fruits or melons we could find to quench our indescribable hunger.

In our tiny village out in the country, there were maybe twenty houses, each separated by roughly 500 meters, or a little more than a quarter of a mile. When I was born in 1961, Venezuela produced more than 10 percent of the world's crude oil, and its economy was booming as a result.

While others in the country might have been flush with cash, that wasn't true for my family or my community.

REBEL LEADERSHIP

Growing up in what has been described as the poorest section of the nation, our family lived in a small house with four walls made of clay, a floor made of sand, and sheets of zinc metal for a ceiling. I'll never forget my mother throwing buckets of water onto the floor so the sand wouldn't fly up and dust fill our nostrils. She cooked our meals on a wood fire. It was very primitive. At the time, our family was made up of my father, Luis Urdaneta, my mother, Euda Fuenmayor, and three boys, who would eventually number seven in the years that followed. Money didn't define us, nor did the lack of it keep us from being happy.

When I was born, my father was still studying to become a teacher and my mother stayed home to take care of the kids. After my father graduated, the Venezuelan government built a school with two classrooms in front of our house so he could teach first and second grades. Growing up, we saw how my mother and my father were fighting to overcome their precarious situation. I saw how hard my father worked, day and night, to be able to get his teaching degree. But despite his hard work, we still faced substantial economic and financial limitations. My parents did everything they could to cover all the needs we had in the house. But it was never enough. We were always in debt. When my family eventually moved to the city, my parents bought a home with a loan.

DREAMING IN VENEZUELA

I remember receiving letters with ultimatums saying we either needed to pay or leave the home. It finally reached a point where we couldn't do proper maintenance on the house anymore. When it stormed, there would be an infiltration of rain into the house. I remember on several occasions waking up as the sun was just starting to rise and we had to get up and grab buckets to take the water out of the house.

I'll never forget one Sunday around that time when my mother sat me and my brothers down. "We don't have any food in the house right now and we're going to go to your aunt and uncle's to visit. There is a good chance we can get something to eat there," she said. "Now, never say that you're hungry and never say that you want them to give you food. If they offer it to us, perfect. But nobody should ask for food." That was a big lesson at thirteen years old. On more than one occasion, we would go to our aunt's house just to be able to eat. It was very difficult for me to see my parents in that situation, to see how hard they were fighting but still not able to carry that load.

My mother and father had financial limitations, but they didn't have limitations on creating more children. I often joke: Why did my parents have seven kids? Because we didn't have a TV. In reality, that joke is only partially true — my parents had more children even after

REBEL LEADERSHIP

we moved to the city and got a television! ☺

My family was one without economic resources, but it was not a family without values. My mother and father taught me that even with limitations, you could achieve great things. We all have had to face limitations in our families or situations. It's up to us to feed our desire to be better. You don't get to choose where you come from or how you are born. You're where you are in life because you were meant to be there, but you don't have to stay. At some point we have two options in life. We can choose the pathway of success or we can choose the pathway of failure. We can model the good or we can model the bad. I had the option to simply say I was born poor, and I could continue being poor. But I also had the option of modeling myself after those people who overcame adversities to achieve their goals.

This is important: in my opinion, there's poor in terms of money and then there are poor minds. I was born poor in terms of money but I did not have a poor mind. What I admired most about my mother was that even though she didn't know how to read or write, those limitations never made her believe, at any point in her life, that she wasn't able to make it. Learning how to model conduct that inspires you to achieve your goals is very important. If you start modeling or copying good conduct, then you can start changing your life. It doesn't matter where you are now, the circumstances you face, or your age. If you understand that you can change your vision and model appropriate conduct, you can achieve your dreams.

DREAMING BIG

Some of the most valuable lessons my mother taught me from a very young age were to love work, fight for what you want, and, although there are many things you don't like, to do them *now*, without hesitation. My mother taught me the trade of sales without knowing that it would become my great passion.

She may not have known how to read or write, but by being bold, brave, and fearless, my mother was able to help my father raise their seven children. My mother's fighting spirit inspired me, and the education that my mother gave us about how to be disciplined and work hard for what we wanted was also really important. While my father worked long hours running the school, my mother did what she could while raising me and my brothers at home. She cooked a very typical food called *bollitos*, or tamales as they call it in many other countries, and my older brother and I were in charge of selling them. They were so delicious. On Saturday mornings, with bags of food in hand, my brother and I would leave home with our neighbor, a woman who worked at a psychiatric hospital in Maracaibo. When we arrived, we went floor by floor selling the bollitos on credit to the nurses. One Saturday we would sell the food and the next Saturday we would go back to sell more and collect payments from the week before. We sold them not only in the hospitals but also to our neighbors. My mother learned how to do a bit of everything in the kitchen to feed our family and bring in some money however she could. She even learned how to prepare cakes for birthday party celebrations. It wasn't a lot, but it added to the family budget. My mother was teaching me to be a fighter. On any weekend when we didn't have to sell food at the hospital, my older brother and I had to wake up early to help my mother clean the house. We had to mop, dust, and sweep the patio. On one hand, my mother needed us to help her. But on the other hand, she was educating us in our responsibilities. Those situations were very important for my brothers and me, but in particular for me, because they helped me understand how to move forward in difficult situations when I was barely a teenager.

When I was growing up, my grandfather had a house that was surrounded by fields where he grew fruits and legumes. In our free time, we would help him cultivate the crops — and maybe eat some too. I don't think my father and my mother knew what they were doing during those moments. They thought they were getting support

DREAMING IN VENEZUELA

from me and my brothers to help carry us forward, but they didn't realize they were actually teaching us to be fighters. When I saw my father and mother working with so much dedication, they were teaching me. They were subconsciously our professors. I modeled myself after them.

As I shared stories with a good friend recently, he wondered, "A man who comes from a very poor family, who didn't study in a university, and who was living in a low-income neighborhood. What did they put in your head?" I believe the seed my mother and father planted in my head was hard work and the ability to dream big, no matter your circumstances. Life didn't come easy for my parents, but they always strived for a better life. It's true that it's not easy to wish for something you don't know. When I was young, I didn't dream of a billion-dollar business. My dreams were simpler. I dreamed of getting out of financial mediocrity, of changing the trajectory of my family.

For me, dreaming is about vision and breaking the paradigms that society teaches us ever since we are born: study, go to college, graduate, find a good job, and make your family. That's a normal and common thing to do. They never tell you to educate yourself and try to be an entrepreneur. That's the difference between staying where you are or charting a new path. Some people break those rules and have different visions. Other people tell themselves, *I'm not going to risk what is secure. I want to be paid on the first and the fifteenth.* It's easier to fall into that mindset where most people are born within that paradigm. It makes you afraid to leave one thing to go for something else that isn't as secure. It creates fear to take the risk. Growing up in Venezuela, I needed to take the risk to create a better future. You cannot live a relaxed life and have big things. That does not exist. If you take the risk, you can achieve and aspire for better things. But you must take those risks. You *can* make it as a square peg in a round hole.

One of the strongest traits throughout my life has been the ability to dream big and to visualize my dreams. I don't know where it comes from, but dreaming for me has always been like making a movie inside my head. What drives me in life is to achieve whatever I created and saw in that movie. It's about making those movies into a plan and doing whatever it takes to achieve it. You can't let go of the movie. And when one movie is almost over, my mind begins to create something different, a new movie with *bigger* dreams. It shifts to starting the *next* screenplay.

Think about what movie is running in your head. Is it the right movie? Should it be a better movie? Do you even *have* a movie? If not, what dreams excite you?

DREAMING IN VENEZUELA

If it's about the money, then you're in the wrong place. This needs to go beyond the money. Because if you start working only because of material things, there's no passion. There's no love. Without passion it is almost impossible to achieve short- or long-term objectives, regardless of the obstacles and difficulties that arise along the way. You have had — or will have — to do things that you don't like or that are not economically convenient for you, but if those activities or challenges are on the path of your dreams, do not hesitate to start down the path now. Do not waste time.

If you find yourself stuck and the movie never changes, it gets boring. When you feel stuck, it may be time to refresh your movie. The one who doesn't change their movie is the one who loses the goal. Don't let your hunger die — ever. There always has to be passion, and we always need to want more. Character, passion, perseverance, and hunger are what really matter to achieve our dreams. Many people strive hard for their dreams, but without these characteristics, even if they make an effort, it doesn't work. A person's effort can be big and permanent, but without these four qualities, the effort isn't worth it. Anyone can achieve what he or she wants if they work hard and don't surrender.

That is to say, talent is made. But talent alone is never enough to succeed. Even when you develop talent, if you don't educate your behaviors and take advantage of it, it becomes useless. That's why there are so many talented people who aren't successful — because they don't take advantage of their other virtues. They lean *only* on their talent. There are very talented people in this world who don't achieve the things they could or should. Even if their talent is excellent, they don't reach their goals because they lack discipline or focus. Through my journey, I didn't have all the talent, but I had the character, passion, perseverance, and hunger, and I had the focus. That was stronger than having talent. I've always tried to develop my talent, but I believe those qualities are more important than talent itself.

If you want to dream big, you need to work hard for it. You cannot have one without the other. There will be stress along the way depending on how big your dream is. Some people might kill their dream, saying, "I just want a job, a good car, a good house, and a beautiful family because I don't want any stress." And there is nothing wrong with that, but it's important to know there is more than that. For the majority of people, that's normal. There are a lot of people who aren't willing to pay that price and they settle for small thinking. You can dream big, but you don't make it without the appropriate actions. You can't lose that spirit. You have to always be looking and looking and looking for that movie. Never settle, never stay calm, keep dreaming, and keep going until you finish that movie — then start another one.

Until you die, you have to learn to keep on learning. That is the truth of what has happened in my life. For as long as I can remember, I've been learning. Learning from failure, learning from adversity, learning to dream, learning to dominate fear. Something I say a lot is that you have to really dream and to believe that dream. Many people say, "I dream! I dream that tomorrow I can achieve my greatest success." But they are lying to themselves because when the time for action comes, they don't take action because they surrender or because they're lazy. Those are not real dreams. When the dream is for real, it inspires you, it motivates you, it moves you into action.

CHOOSING A DIFFERENT PATH

Around the time my oldest brother was finishing elementary school in Las Cuatro Bocas, my mother told my father that we needed to move to the city. There was no high school in our rural neighborhood so moving closer to the city was the only way for my brother to keep learning. My father was always very firm in his belief that it was crucial to be educated to be able to overcome our situation. He always taught us we had to study so we could prepare for better opportunities.

REBEL LEADERSHIP

Still, my father didn't want to go. My grandfather and other relatives lived nearby, and moving to the city would mean our immediate family would have to go alone. My mother was always a strong woman, and in that time of transition she was very firm. She didn't push my father — she *forced* him to go to the city. And so, when I was ten years old, we moved to a new neighborhood east of Maracaibo called La Rotaria. It was a beautiful neighborhood and one of the most beautiful stages of my life. Growing up in the small village, we didn't have any neighbors, but when we moved to Street 82 in the city, the houses sat one next to the other. We lived in a small concrete house and we had a big yard; there was a baseball stadium one street over and a basketball hoop on our road. It was a neighborhood that after some time became part of our family. There were kids my age and we all grew up together, going to school, of course, but also spending time in the streets. We were all like one family and we helped each other out.

I think an important quality in life is the ability to observe, to see and digest the good things in life, even if we're not in the best situation. One thing that truly marked me was that even when we left our home in the village and moved to the city, we lived in a very small three-room house. But we had a house that was comfortable and made our quality of life better. Watching my father continuously developing himself as a teacher and my mother cooking food to help our family, I saw the sacrifices they made for a better life.

I have to confess that I wasn't very good with my studies. I had too many dreams in my mind. I didn't like school; I didn't like going, and when I went, I was quite a rebel. All my siblings were good students but not me. I was always a headache for my mom and my dad. When we went to school, we were required to wear dark blue pants, a white polo shirt, and white tennis shoes. I would put on anything I could find that weren't the tennis shoes because I knew my teacher would get angry and I wanted to see her lose control. I liked it! I was a rebel, but I was also very clumsy. I wanted to stand out, so I would search for fights with other kids. I lost them all. The school would call my mom about my rebellious behavior, and I was suspended on more than one occasion. At that age I was already looking for girlfriends, but nobody wanted to be my girlfriend because I was the worst behaved kid in the class and I was a bad student. Who wanted to be with a loser?

When I was fourteen, I told my parents I was done going to school, that I was going to work instead. My father got really angry. "You have to finish," he demanded. I was practically forced to finish.

One day nearing the end of high school, my brother, parents, and I were gathered in front of our house with my uncle, who turned to my father to say, "Wow, Luis. Edixon is a great student. You have Leonardo, Jesus, and Omar, who are very good students. The only one who isn't graduating is Luis. He's not studying." My uncle turned and pointed at me. "What do you feel, Luis, seeing yourself as a good-for-nothing?" I remember those words like it was yesterday. There are some moments in which those kind of comments will bring a person down. But other times, those comments will be inspiring. Everything depends on how you see your own difficult moments. The reason I never forgot that moment isn't because I feel resentment or bitterness but because at sixteen, it inspired me and left a mark on me to prove to my uncle that he was mistaken. *One day I will show him that I am capable of doing whatever he thinks I am not capable of doing*, I thought.

I want you to put this in your mind and on your heart; it's something that became a premise and the statement of my life: don't let anyone steal your dreams.

CHAPTER 3

CHASING OPPORTUNITIES

I TALK A LOT about perseverance and its cousin, persistence. You must have the mental strength to make your way through tough spots and then the grit to stick with the decisions you know are right.

My stated goal of putting school aside so I could enter the world of work finally paid off during my third year of high school. "I don't want to continue studying during the day," I told my mother and father. "I'll finish high school during the night. But during the day, I'll go to work." With some reluctance, they finally gave me permission to start looking for a daytime job.

I didn't have a lot of options, but I had heard there was an opportunity at a shoe store in the center of the city, and I was given a job as a salesperson. That was the first store that offered me a chance, and it gave me the

REBEL LEADERSHIP

option of working during the day and studying at night. That way I could finish high school, which was what my father wanted, but I could begin to earn a little money for myself, which was my goal. So at sixteen years old, I started working during the day selling shoes. That's where I earned my first "real" paycheck, even if it wasn't much. At that time in my life, I was very shy, which isn't the best trait when your job is to put shoes on people's feet. I was the worst salesperson. The shoe store was family owned, and the owners created a competitive environment. They prized the employees who had the best results, and I learned to always want to win and to always want to be the best. And yet I never was. The store was in the city center and hundreds of people walked past the storefront on their way to work. The goal was to stand on the sidewalk out front and grab these people's attention, get them inside the store, and hopefully sell them a pair of shoes. Imagine me, an extreme introvert in my first real job . . . I wanted to die. It was very difficult, but wanting to make money and keep my bosses happy, I knew I had to do it no matter how much I hated it. Knowing there was competition and prizes for the best salesperson helped me break those fears too. Even if I wasn't very good at convincing people, at least I dared to search for customers and tried to get them into the store. I was always inspired by competition.

CHASING OPPORTUNITIES

That was one of many lessons I learned at the shoe store. It's important to have that competitive spirit and to get people to dream about their goals. The husband and wife who owned the store were never happy or satisfied even with big achievements. They were always praising us, but they were constantly asking for more. Even in my adolescence, those were experiences and lessons that stuck with me. They were extremely demanding with their sales staff, and those who didn't meet their standards were let go. It was important to me to be able to maintain my employment. Maybe it wasn't normal to rationalize it this way as a teenager, but I knew that if the woman felt good grace towards me, her husband would not fire me. That's exactly what happened. The wife liked me, and it opened doors. I was selling shoes, but I ended up learning leadership along the way. I was always looking for human connection in those transformative years. I knew if I connected with a person, I would have better opportunities. Maybe this is where I learned to always push for more, to always be on the lookout for what was next.

As I've gotten older, I've wondered, *Is a leader born or is a leader developed?* I'm convinced that leadership is developed. Going back to the skill of making a connection with the owner of the shoe store, I learned that lesson from the time my mother sent me to sell food at the psychiatric hospital. When I purchased food at the market for my mother to cook when I was barely twelve years old, it helped me to start forming leadership qualities and to overcome my fears because I had responsibilities that were not meant for a twelve-year-old child. I learned that when you empower other people, you have a better chance of developing their leadership qualities than when you're trying to do all the work of the people you are responsible for. My mother helped me learn leadership skills and self-motivation, both of which are crucial to being able to achieve the objectives that you want to reach in life.

I worked at the shoe store for about a year until I finished high school. When I graduated high school and went to pick up my degree, I noticed there was one subject that I didn't pass from the third year of high school. They couldn't give me the degree and were forcing me to go back to school to retake English, which I hadn't passed. Here I was at a stage in my life where I thought I was finally liberated from what I didn't want to do. When the school told me that I had to go back and do the entire English class for third year over again, I said, "No, let's leave it as it is. I'm not interested. I don't want to have anything to do with school anymore." It was an interesting moment in my life because my father totally disagreed with my decision.

CHASING OPPORTUNITIES

"My son," he said disappointedly, "you don't want to study and your brother is already going to the university."

"Dad, I'm going to promise you something," I told him. "I'm not going to study again. I'm going to work. I'm going to fight hard. And I can assure and promise you that when my older brother graduates from college, I'm going to have my own business. When he graduates, I will be a very successful entrepreneur."

TOUCHING DINERO

What's ironic about my story is that when I was finally freed from studying and going to school, someone told me about a course offered by the small, local bank to become an employee. The difference was, the bank was going to provide a monthly payment to take the course and I could visualize an opportunity down the road. Being able to count money got my attention. I thought, *If I'm working in a bank, I can be a cashier, and being a cashier, I will be able to touch money. It's not mine, but at least I will touch it.* So I decided to go after my next opportunity.

I completed the course and was hired by the bank. The only problem was, I wasn't hired as a cashier like I wanted because I wasn't quite eighteen and was too young. Instead, I was hired in the accounting department where we'd we received and published the correspondence between banks for each transaction. It was boring work, but I knew it was a door for me to enter to get where I ultimately wanted to go. So each day around noon, I would take my lunch break, eat as fast as I could, and help the cashiers. I knew that if I did a good job there and if I supported the cashiers, management would give me an opportunity. My efforts paid off and the bank made me a cashier assistant until eventually I became a cashier after a few months. I was able to achieve my goal, which was counting money. You have to be focused on what you truly want, and if you're focused on that all the time, a path will open up. I wasn't happy in the department I was in, but I knew that a path could open up if I kept the correct focus.

I enjoyed handling money for a little while, but after spending time counting money — the monetary denomination is the bolívares in Venezuela — I realized it didn't fulfill me because it wasn't *my* money. I had reached my goal, but even if I could count bolívares every day, the pay for a cashier was very low. More importantly, I realized it wasn't my True North. That's when I realized I had to start searching for new alternatives. Today these kinds of "opportunities" are known to most people as "side hustles." Trust me, I was willing to hustle!

I let friends know I was open to new opportunities,

CHASING OPPORTUNITIES

and they began to open up in interesting ways. During that time, the bolívares was really strong and the Colombian peso was weak. Because of this, someone told me there was good business in buying cigarettes in Colombia and smuggling them into Venezuela. To transport the cigarettes across the border from Colombia to Venezuela, I needed to hide them in the vehicle. But with my desire for opportunities in business, I dared to try. I got a loan from my neighbor to buy a few cases of cigarettes, and at eighteen years old I started driving west toward the northeastern Colombian border. When I reached the Colombian border to enter Venezuela on my way home, the border patrol officer found the hidden cigarettes and took all of them and the remaining money I had gotten as a loan. It's an experience that I laugh about today, but the truth is that I was left with debt and the challenge of paying the money back. I only tried smuggling once. Still, there was a valuable lesson there. Taking that trip was all about searching for opportunity. To find an opportunity or to go down a new pathway in life, you have to overcome the fear of losing money and overcome the fear of failing. As I've learned many times in my life, the only way you can do those two things is by trying, failing, and losing. People might look at me today and wonder, *How did he get there?* The truth is, I've been failing since I was sixteen. Some people wait until they're thirty to start their own business or search for new opportunities. I've failed and lost since I was a teenager. My story is one of messing up until I made it. That has given me an advantage. When people experience losing from an early age, they grow a thick skin. "OK, I lost some money. I'll make it again. I can fail, learn from it, and try again." You're going to become successful at some point.

My failure at the Colombian border didn't deter me from seeking out new opportunities. In fact, it only made me more daring to always search for the best opportunity. Around the same time, I met an Italian man who owned a restaurant in Maracaibo. He also sold heavy machinery for agriculture. My ability to get on people's good side helped me, and the Italian man was sympathetic to me. As I searched for my next step, I helped him purchase food for his restaurant. One day he said, "I need to send a machine to Sabana de Mendoza. I have nobody to send the machine with. Would you know how to do it?" Always daring and looking for opportunity, I said, "Of course I can." The truth was, I didn't know where the town of Sabana de Mendoza was, and I didn't even have a driver's license. But he said he would pay me for the trip, so I helped him load the machine on the company truck and I began driving in the general direction of my destination. Sabana de Mendoza was 215 kilometers (about 135 miles) across the channel near Maracaibo

CHASING OPPORTUNITIES

and straight south. Back in the 1980s, there was no GPS. No nothing! I knew I had to take a particular road, but I had no idea where Sabana de Mendoza was. The man gave me money for gas and food, and I was on my way. About halfway down what turned out to be Highway 17, the police stopped me and asked for my driving license documents. I didn't have any. In Venezuela, it was very easy to bribe an officer with $5 or $10 and they would let you go. I started talking to the officer and explained that this was a job that I was doing for my boss and if I didn't do it, he was going to fire me. "I have a bit of money here to give you so you can let me go," I told him. It was all the money I had to eat. Of course, he let me go. After stopping several times along the way to ask for directions, I finally arrived in Sabana de Mendoza. I spent a hungry day on the road, but I was able to achieve my objective and learned a valuable lesson: you have to be daring.

MY OWN BOSS

That daring attitude is what led to my first son, Ray, being born in February 1981 when I was nineteen years old. Becoming a father at a young age forced me to grow up and take chances in order to support my family. Yes, back then I was even daring in that. I always said there's no better college than the streets. Those experiences broke a lot of my fears. But nothing could have prepared me for fatherhood as a teenager.

To help support our small family, I decided to go off on my own. My then father-in-law gave me a small piece of land in front of my in-laws' house to open a little kiosk, almost like a small supermarket, which is very popular in Latin America. For the first time, I didn't have a boss. My kiosk was a tiny little thing. I don't think I had even $200. It was something that, truthfully, wasn't worth a lot, but my dream was precisely to make it grow. I would go to the market to stock up on items to sell, essential items such as toothpaste, rice, and milk for babies. Sometimes in one day, three or four customers would buy from my stand. Most of the time, I sat there waiting for someone to come. Usually it was the neighbors. After a while, I decided to purchase a small refrigerator so I could start selling meat, chicken, and other perishables. But the business didn't go well because those products expired fast. I operated the kiosk for about four months before I called it quits, realizing my small income wasn't enough to help me move ahead on the path I was chasing, which was to get out of the precarious financial situation we were in to search for opportunities that would change my quality of life. I've said that you always need to have a reason "why." That "why" is your inspiration to overcome any failure. I believe that when you have a very powerful

CHASING OPPORTUNITIES

"why" you will be able to overcome obstacles, failures, and adversities. Ray became one of my strongest inspirations to fight and to search for my opportunities. He became my biggest "why." When Ray was born, I had someone who was feeding my dreams.

I've always thought that to discover new opportunities and find success, you have to be hungry all the time. In many cases, that comes from having a "why" that drives your every move. You have to be careful. If you don't fall in love with what you do, if you're not passionate about it, and if you don't believe in it, you're in the wrong place because you're never going to get it — or at least you'll never be satisfied.

What I knew in early 1981 was that my business wasn't working and the money wasn't enough. I had grand dreams and a relentless hunger that kept me searching for the next opportunity. As my kiosk trickled out a small income, I watched one day as my childhood neighbor pulled up to his house in a nice, new vehicle. He said he had earned it in direct sales. "You can also earn it," he told me. Now he had my attention.

I had touched money. I had gotten a taste of business. Now I had new expectations and a new hunger: how do I make *real* money?

CHAPTER 4

TWO PINK BAGS

GROWING UP in Venezuela, I never understood a popular saying in my town that the older people often repeated. *Dicen que todo inicio es duro y penoso.* Translated, it means, "They say that every beginning is hard and painful."

When I saw my friend Ivan Mora pull up across the street from my parents' home in La Rotaria driving a nice, new car, it gave me my first glimpse at what was possible. I had grown up playing with Ivan in the streets and now he told me about a direct sales business called Tupperware where you could earn a new vehicle, you could earn money, and you could travel the world. I started building new expectations, a new hunger that I'd never experienced. Ivan invited me to my first Tupperware meeting the following Monday, and while I wasn't so sure about direct sales or the promises he claimed, I decided to take him up on the offer and tag along.

That Monday morning when I walked into the big

REBEL LEADERSHIP

warehouse, it felt almost like listening to a pastor giving a sermon at church. There were roughly one hundred people gathered for the recruiting meeting. There were ninety-eight women and two men — me and Ivan. "This isn't for me," I told Ivan. "This is crazy! This is for women." I didn't feel comfortable, but Ivan persuaded me to stay. He said it was also for men and that eventually the husbands of Tupperware's leading distributors would come, too, but no other men showed up that day. When it was over, I wasn't convinced that I would ever go back to one of the meetings. Ray's mother, my wife at the time, lived with my parents, where we had a room for Ray. When we returned home that night, my mother was really upset. "You're not going to do that kind of business," she told me strongly. "That business is *not* for men!" She said I should stay away from Tupperware, telling me I didn't belong there. I wasn't even sure I liked the idea of direct sales — of knocking on doors and selling to homemakers — but I saw the opportunity. At the time, it was a difficult lesson that I had to learn by disappointing my mother and going against her wishes. You have to be careful with the negative people who you have around you in your life, even the people closest to you. I tell people that in many cases, the enemy, the most negative one — the black cloud — is often in your own house. What helped me overcome that negativity was the fact that I believed more in the dream

TWO PINK BAGS

of earning a new vehicle and the other opportunities that direct sales offered my family and me than how others might perceive me. I chose to let myself be guided by the instinct of searching for a great opportunity.

My life in this newfound business called Tupperware didn't get any easier when I signed up and Ivan presented me with two pink bags, the trademark carrying cases that salespeople used to tote around their Tupperware products when demonstrating at their personal sales meetings. I was already on edge after Ivan and I had been surrounded by ninety-eight women at my introduction meeting to Tupperware and my mother had pleaded with me to do something different. Now the company had decided that the bags sellers would carry to demo their products would be *pink*. Since I didn't have a vehicle at that time, I had to leave home most nights around 6 p.m. to catch the bus to my meetings. Every time I left the house, I had to walk past my neighbors, the ones I had grown up with playing baseball and basketball against in the street. Of course, I left with those two pink bags. You can imagine the mocking and bullying I endured from my friends. As I boarded the city bus and struggled to my seat, everybody stared at me and my two pink bags. I was a young man coming of age with a son. It was a very, very difficult experience but one I felt was necessary to get ahead with my dreams.

What I learned is you don't have to be afraid of the pink bag and you cannot be intimidated by the naysayers trying to make you think that you're going down the wrong path.

Those two pink bags taught me a valuable lesson: Never be afraid of what people think or say. Never be afraid to carry a pink bag when working on making your dreams a reality.

DOING THE UNCOMFORTABLE

Just off the shore of Lago de Maracaibo, a large inlet that extends 210 kilometers (about 130 miles) and connects Zulia State's capital city to the Caribbean Sea, is Plaza Baralt, where I observed and learned the trade of direct sales and began my own career.

Shortly after I received my two pink bags and demonstration products, I made my way to the busy plaza to observe the crowd. Across the square I saw two people successfully building connections and selling Tupperware. I moved closer to the young couple and worked up the courage to interrupt. "How do you do it?" I asked. That's how I met Rosibel and Hugo. They explained their process to me, and it sounded almost like a broken record. *Go to the plaza, knock on doors, go to the plaza, knock on doors; train, motivate, train, motivate.* I began following

TWO PINK BAGS

right behind them. Everything they did, I did. Eventually, we would compete with one another when I became a distributor; they were two of the best Tupperware distributors in the city but amidst the competition we began to travel and spend time with one another. I told myself, *I need to hang around people who are successful.* I don't know where that instinct came from, but from the beginning I always tried to get to know the best Tupperware leaders in Maracaibo. In those early days, I didn't build my own business in Tupperware because I had great knowledge but because I *absorbed* knowledge from the people who did it best. My then-wife and I were always focused on observing successful people and learning from people who were the best.

When I started in Tupperware and direct sales in 1982, I had absolutely no idea what the world was about. More than wanting to be the top salesperson at the national level in Venezuela or even locally in Maracaibo, I felt a strong desire to understand and develop my own Tupperware business. In those days I wasn't merely thinking about being the best; I was thinking about how I could take advantage of the opportunity that was being given to me and make it successful. I searched for any opportunity to sharpen my skills.

That search led me, an introverted young man, to approach Rosibel and Hugo on Plaza Baralt that day,

REBEL LEADERSHIP

beginning a relationship that taught me my first lessons in direct sales. Not long after, I made an important observation: Rosibel and Hugo were good friends with the #1 Tupperware distributors in Maracaibo, a married couple named Nora and Alfonso Rodriguez. Many weekends, the two couples would meet at Nora and Alfonso's home, where they would eat, drink, and talk business. I wanted to meet the Rodriguezes badly. "How can I become friends with Nora and Alfonso?" I asked Hugo. "It's very hard," he told me. What made it harder was that I wasn't a super social person. Still, I made it clear to Rosibel and Hugo that I wanted to join the two couples some weekend. One Friday, after posting good sales results, I finally received an invitation. *This is my opportunity*, I told myself. *I cannot lose this opportunity*. I was determined not only to win the visit (by having them like me), but to be invited back. I knew I needed to do things that made them feel like they needed me around.

As we sat on Nora and Alfonso's patio that Friday afternoon, I paid attention to everything. I was timid, but I wanted to learn. So I just sat there and listened. Nora smoked, and I noticed she ran out of cigarettes. "I can go buy more cigarettes for you," I offered. Later, as we sat around and drank, we ran out of beer. "I'll go get some more," I said. That evening, Nora said she needed to get their son from the university. "I'll pick him up," I told her.

TWO PINK BAGS

I was completely out of my comfort zone, but I spoke up because I knew it would help build a connection. In today's world, there is a trend of not doing things that are uncomfortable. So many people go along in life with the mindset, *If it's uncomfortable or if it doesn't feel right, don't do it*. If you live life with that mindset, then how do you get to where you want to be? I learned then, and still preach it in meetings with my team today, that in search of success, in search of opportunities, you have to learn to do the things that you like as well as the things you don't like. I didn't like riding the bus or walking around Maracaibo with a bag conducting home parties, much less with bags that were pink! I had to do it. There was no alternative. It didn't feel good to go to somebody else's house and serve them in the hope that they would find me useful and invite me back, but I felt that those actions were the ones that were going to open a new path. I tried to find ways for Nora and Alfonso to realize I was useful, even if it was as simple as picking up the things they needed. I don't know if that was what worked or not, but from that day forward they invited me to their house every week.

Those weekends on the patio were the best direct sales workshops I could have ever asked for. Nora and Alfonso would prepare meals, we'd sit on the patio with drinks, and, of course, the conversation was always about the Tupperware business. While we were drinking beer we talked about their experiences, which were filled with success, but also about the experiences of their peers and what was not successful. I dedicated myself to absorbing everything they talked about because I knew they were the two best distributors not only in Maracaibo but in all of Venezuela. Those conversations gave me the knowledge not only of what should be done to be successful in direct sales but also what should not be done.

Those weekend get-togethers reminded me that to be successful in direct sales, I had to go out and find opportunities myself. There were two ways of doing that. The first was to go to Plaza Baralt, where a statue of Rafael María Baralt was surrounded by Maracaibo Cathedral and Baralt Theatre, two cornerstones of Maracaibo where people would gather. I searched for a busy area and laid a tablecloth across my space on the plaza, placing all of my Tupperware on top for people to see as they walked past. It was one of the most difficult moments I experienced. Although an introvert, I had started to break through my fears, but standing on the plaza with my products on the ground trying to draw the attention of each passerby was uncomfortable. I didn't like going to the plaza to demonstrate Tupperware to find potential customers who might be interested in the products, but I had heard Nora and Alfonso say it was the key to getting more clients. As someone walked past, I would encourage them to come

TWO PINK BAGS

close, almost like a salesperson in the mall who tries to capture the attention of each passerby and draw them in with a free sample. I wasn't actually trying to sell them Tupperware. The goal was to schedule appointments to arrange a gathering in their homes. In many cases, it was humiliating. People were rude. There were times I would call out to people and they wouldn't even look at me. People looked down on me because I was selling. There was nothing I could do but accept it.

The second way to create selling opportunities was to knock on doors. If I wasn't on Plaza Baralt demonstrating the products, I could be found in neighborhoods around Maracaibo knocking on doors with my two pink bags and a sales pitch. "I come to offer you the opportunity to obtain marvelous products that I can give to you as a present if you just give me the opportunity to explain to you how you and I can build something interesting," I told them. If I knocked on a hundred doors, ten opened. Of those ten, maybe two would say *yes.* The entire goal was to get a meeting so I could add people to my sales team. Some doors wouldn't open, while other doors opened only to be shut right in my face. But I had heard in the meetings with Nora and Alfonso that knocking on doors was a key to success. They said if one door didn't open, knock on the next door, and if that door didn't open, search for another door until at least one of the doors opened and that person agreed to host a home party. I didn't like doing it. There were many things I didn't like doing, but I realized each one of those things I didn't like gave me the results to be able to achieve my objectives. I understood that I had to force myself to do the uncomfortable if I wanted to achieve big results.

Over time, I began to lose my fear of rejection. The few people who stopped to hear my sales pitch on the plaza or who opened the door to their home and listened offered the hope of opportunity. That is how everything was built. It was the start of my base, the foundation to be where I am now.

LOSING THE FEAR OF REJECTION

When I started in Tupperware, it was as a husband with my wife as the salesperson. In the early days, I would accompany my wife to home parties, and when they ended, I would go around picking up. I did the practical work. When I met Rosibel and Hugo, I realized that Hugo organized his own meetings and Rosibel organized hers. That's when I told myself, *Okay, I'm going to dare to do it.* That is what happens when you meet successful people — you want to copy their success.

It was an uncomfortable hill to climb, but I finally decided to do it. One day, I called my cousin Aritza and

TWO PINK BAGS

she agreed to organize a Tupperware party at her home. I was a nervous wreck when I arrived at her home and then demonstrated my Tupperware products in front of the eight other women. I had watched during the meetings my wife had done and I learned from her, but I didn't have all the Tupperware products memorized yet. I practiced my demonstration before the meeting and wrote the names of each product underneath so I could remember them. I knew everything I needed to do and then once the meeting started . . . I forgot it all. It was like the stage fright and nerves made my mind go blank. I was so nervous that I forgot to check the names I had written on the bottoms of each product. As I was holding the Tupperware product for storing salads and vegetables, I panicked. I couldn't think of its name. I had to get creative fast to make sure people didn't know what was happening. "Let's do a competition," I said. "Who can tell me the name of this product?" After a pause, somebody shouted out, "La Fresquita!" I breathed a sigh of relief. "Marvelous," I said with a smile, "you know the name!" By the time I left Aritza's home, I had managed to make a sale and schedule two future Tupperware parties.

When I got home, I celebrated and handed my wife a piece of paper. "Here are the addresses so you can go and host the meetings," I told her. When she called the two customers I had scheduled parties with, they both told her that if I wasn't going to be there, then they weren't going to organize the parties. That was a moment of inspiration I needed. I led those two meetings myself and continued doing more and more. From then on, I was free. When I started in Tupperware, my self-esteem was low. I had been a poor student and had never been recognized positively in my early life. When I started receiving positive recognition, it proved powerful. They inspired me, knowing I was valuable, and that there were people who believed in me. It was those moments that helped me give more and more of myself to the business every day. During Tupperware's Monday morning meetings, which now had about three hundred leaders in attendance, I started being publicly recognized for my accomplishments. For me, it was an uplifting experience. Of course, when someone starts being praised and recognized, that person wants to have that sweet taste in their mouth permanently. Those early experiences are the ones that make me tell leaders now, "When you start in direct sales, you're searching for money. But in that search for money, when you start receiving recognition from your work, money comes in second place because recognition starts inspiring you even more than the money."

I didn't like doing exhibitions in town squares. I didn't like knocking on doors. I didn't like home demonstrations.

TWO PINK BAGS

But that's what I had to do to be able to thrive in my situation. I learned that if you limit yourself to doing only what you like, you won't be able to get the maximum potential of the opportunity that you have before you. Without doing all of those things I initially despised, I would be just another one of thousands of salespeople in Venezuela.

That doesn't mean it was easy. Even when I seemingly managed to interest people on the plaza enough to proceed with a planning meeting for a house party, and they gave me the address to their homes, when I searched for the address, it was often fake. Only a small percentage was real. So at the end of a long day of work, I would have to convince the few whose addresses were real to organize a meeting in their home. Of course, in that world in 1980s Venezuela, sexism was even stronger. On many occasions when I knocked on doors, women would accept the proposal to do the home meeting. But when the time came to meet, I would be told, "My husband doesn't want you in the house." It was a constant battle of rejection and a difficult start. But I chose to be fueled by success instead of being dismayed by rejection.

What I had learned from my mother at a young age was reinforced in my early days in Tupperware. To be successful, you will do things that you do not like to do. It's up to you to break through barriers that put limits on you to do whatever it is you don't like. Success must be accompanied by sacrifice, and sometimes that means doing things you really don't want to do. Sometimes you have to knock on doors. I didn't like being on the plaza, but I knew I had to do it to be able to get the tools I needed to keep on going ahead with my life. You need to have a purpose. You need to have a "why." Together they can inspire you to deal with any situation.

To be able to achieve and taste success, you're going to find all kinds of challenges, all types of barriers, and all sorts of situations along the way. In the long term, getting to your destination depends on the conviction and the strength of your decision to change your quality of life and achieve a better opportunity every day. On many occasions, people just surrender. That's why the majority doesn't accomplish what the minority achieves. They become worn out with their frustrations, with a demanding of oneself to go an extra mile, and many times, they just don't want to. A lot of people want success, but they aren't willing to sacrifice themselves to be able to reach the finish line.

MY TRUE PASSION

When my first payment in bolívares arrived, I had made more in a week from Tupperware sales than I had ever made in a month as an employee at my previous jobs. Yet

TWO PINK BAGS

while I had started in business to escape financial mediocrity, the money was no longer what inspired me. More than a sale or my weekly paycheck, I started getting that sensation that makes you feel fulfilled, that inspires you, that motivates you, and that makes you break through barriers. Before I started in direct sales, I wasn't noticed for anything. I wasn't a good student. I was a rebel. I was ugly. The only reason anyone noticed me was because I had two pink bags full of Tupperware.

Now, after hours of practice and good results, when I went to group meetings or activities, people started noticing me. I started getting recognized for the results of my sales. That inspired me and made me fall in love with direct sales. I don't even remember how much money I was making because what truly fulfilled me was feeling that people valued me. That's been my flag during all these years since — to make other people feel valued, capable, and appreciated.

As I moved up the ranks in the Tupperware organization, I began to see everything Ivan had told me about back in our neighborhood. On one occasion, the organization bought me a plane ticket to fly across the country to the capital city of Caracas. I remember looking out the window in awe from thirty thousand feet above my country. When I arrived, I was dropped off at a five-star hotel. I had never been in a hotel, and coming from my humble beginnings, that experience was marvelous. That trip marked me in many ways. I remember they would say, "Doors open at 7 p.m." And right on the dot, the doors opened at 7 p.m. When they said, "Event closes at 9 p.m.," you could be sure it ended right at 9 p.m. That stuck with me because nowadays I am obsessed with punctuality and excellence in every aspect of my life. I learned that from my Tupperware business.

    I'll never forget the day I ranked up in Tupperware and earned a vehicle. It was a small, two-door, white Ford Corsair. I remember driving home and parking it in front of the house. That filled me with satisfaction because those same neighbors who had mocked me for my pink bags could see that it was possible for me to succeed. That's when I started to see my base grow and began convincing my friends and neighbors to join the business. Today two of them are my employees at MONAT. As people in my circle started joining, even my mom was convinced of the opportunity. One day she said, "I want to try too." Yes, what was once a black cloud in my Tupperware dream had now opened up. There is a great truth in this: sometimes we can transform behaviors with results. At first, I hesitated. "You don't know how to write or how to read," I said. "How are you going to do it?" "I'll find a way, son," she told me. My mother was such a fighter. She didn't let either of those deficiencies hold her

TWO PINK BAGS

back. When she went to home parties she would always take my younger sister, Yixa, with her to help schedule the follow-up appointments. Eventually even my mother managed to earn a vehicle. It was proof from her (once again) that limitations do not exist.

To continue having success in direct sales, I couldn't lose my hunger. It was important to never lose the excitement. You need to have a permanent purpose in your mind that will help you defeat adversity to be able to overcome poverty and overcome the behavior of knowing that you don't have money in your bank account, a purpose that inspires you to get out of whatever situation it is that's holding you back. But reaching a milestone doesn't mean you've met your destination. I needed to thrive in my situation so I could have a place to live with my son. After a few months, we were able to move out of my parents' house into our own rented house. We started competing against the best in Tupperware, including Rosibel and Hugo, to see who was the best week after week.

Tupperware and direct sales became my school and my degree. I was motivated by the behaviors and beliefs of the people who said I was good for nothing. I strove every day to prove I was capable. When I turned twenty-three, I did just that. I had my own business in the city just like I had told my father I would. When my younger brother graduated from the university as a civil engineer, I proposed an idea to him: quit your job and come build my house. He built a beautiful home in my city of Maracaibo, and with his earnings he was able to build his own business. The dreams you put into your mind to achieve always have to be active because a mind that settles, a mind that is limited, surrenders too easily. I'm completely convinced that if you educate your mind and your behavior in the appropriate way it will take you past any obstacles to achieve your goals. It's not about the product you're trying to sell, it's not about the business you're in, it's about what you have in your mind. What is your dream? How often are you visualizing it? Do you believe in it? How possible do you really think it is to achieve?

    I lived two stages in direct sales. During my first stage, when Ivan invited me to my first Tupperware meeting, I hated it. I saw direct sales as a means to an end. I felt as if I were being forced to knock on doors and stand on the plaza out of necessity. At first, I admit, it was about the money. When I went to the rallies with other salespeople every Monday, I rolled my eyes. I thought it was ridiculous. You had to dance and do a whole bunch of things I thought were silly and stupid. Then I saw the money and I viewed direct sales as the most beautiful thing in the world. I danced and smiled.

TWO PINK BAGS

The recognition came, and then the opportunity to live a way I had never lived before kept me going. But deep down I knew that those things alone — money and recognition — could never be my why. I needed a passion, a "why," a True North.

When I learned how to develop leadership and saw that I was able to influence other salespeople, generate motivation, and be a guide to help them reach the same results I did, I knew direct sales was my passion. It was no longer just about me. I wanted my own Tupperware team. Something I often reinforce in my conferences is that if you have the appropriate behaviors of a leader and act every day with faith, you will achieve your goals. Do you want to be successful? You need to make other people successful. Do you want to enjoy the success in business and feel happy? Help other people be successful and happy. That became my inspiration and motivation and what guided me into my second stage in Tupperware. There is a saying that I have always believed in: he who sows always reaps. It was time for me to start planting new seeds.

CHAPTER 5

PASSION AND DISCIPLINE: BECOMING #1

THERE IS A PHRASE that says, "You will always remember who was #1, but you won't remember who was #2." At every Monday meeting, Tupperware would recognize the top salespeople, those who delivered the top sales in each category. I followed all of the numbers. At the time, I could tell you who was #1, #2, #3, and so on. If you ask me now who was #2 or #3, I don't remember. Even if #2 had high sales, too, I still couldn't tell you their name. I only remember who was #1.

Being the #1 Tupperware distributor in Venezuela was never my "why," but the leaderboard and weekly reminders helped feed into something I believe is important in any person's journey to success: *to continue having success you must never lose your hunger.* I learned in those early years that the key to never losing the excitement of the fight is to have a permanent purpose. Having your mind set on a purpose will help you defeat adversities and overcome obstacles, a purpose that inspires you to get out of that situation, whatever it might be. One of the things that inspired me when I faced adversity was when Ray was born and I had to work to take care of my son. I needed to thrive in my situation so I could provide a home for my newborn. I didn't want my firstborn child to grow up in the same poverty that I had once experienced. Maybe climbing to the top of the Tupperware leaderboard wasn't my purpose, but it kept me hungry. I saw Nora and Alfonso sitting at #1 on the distributors chart, and Rosibel and Hugo were their top leaders. I saw the opportunities that opened up for them. I was learning from the best, but I wanted to be among them.

    Almost everyone who enters the direct sales industry does so, at least initially, because of the money. I can't lie to you — that was my first instinct too. The reason I attended my first Tupperware meeting as a teenager was because of the allure of what Ivan promised. The car! The trips! The money! Sure, that was all great. My first goal in Tupperware was to escape my family's history of financial mediocrity and chart a new path forward. But if all I ever cared about was the money, that hunger would

PASSION AND DISCIPLINE: BECOMING #1

have died quickly. The fire inside me to keep pressing on in challenging times would have dwindled and eventually burned out, sending me on a different path. Instead, like many others, I began to fall in love with the world of direct sales. Direct sales made me feel like I was transforming people's quality of life for the better and helping them change their habits and mentality. I believe direct sales allowed me to give them a new perspective, and that set them down a new path. That became my driving force. When you fall in love with helping others, it is a blessing from God. That's what made me fall in love with direct sales. The money became something secondary. I learned that if something is only about the money — whatever it is in life — then it's the wrong mindset. Your "why" — your purpose and your hunger — needs to go beyond money. If people work only to gain material possessions, there's no love and no passion. Sure, it might carry a person for a while. But eventually, that person will get stuck in the mud, without hunger or purpose. Maybe you're reading this now realizing you're headed down that very path or, worse, already there, going through the motions each day to get from one paycheck to the next. That's no way to live.

    I said this earlier, but it's worth repeating: *without passion it is almost impossible to achieve your dreams.* What is passion, anyway? I've thrown the word out enough to sound like a broken record, and one might ask, "Luis, how do I know what my passion is?" The Merriam-Webster dictionary defines *passion* "as an intense, driving, or overmastering feeling or conviction." My simplified definition is only three words long: "What inspires you?"

When discussing passion, motivational speaker John C. Maxwell often asks audiences to answer three questions:

What do you sing about?
What do you cry about?
What do you dream about?

Maxwell's reasons to ask these three questions are simple. He says the first two questions help determine what pulls at a person's heart in the present and the third helps define what might fulfill that person in the future.

My children have said that I become obsessed with achieving a goal, and when I want something, I fixate on it. I like to think of it as being passionate. When you have a passion, you can break through limitations. Everybody has a passion inside of him or her — something that sparks a fire, something that makes them emotional. The problem is, many people simply never take time to discover their passion. They say, "I'll do it tomorrow" or "I'll do it later" and continue to be stuck in the same old job or living the same life they want to change only for "tomorrow" or

PASSION AND DISCIPLINE: BECOMING #1

"later" to never come. Why does this happen? Because people don't want to face the unknown and resist change; they're scared they might fail. In his blog post titled "Your Life Can Be a Great Story," Maxwell writes,

To put significance in our stories, we must also take action. Being passive may feel safe. If you do nothing, nothing can go wrong. But while inaction cannot fail, it cannot succeed either. We can wait, and hope, and wish, but if we do, we miss the stories our lives could be. We cannot allow our fears and questions to keep us from starting.

It's easy to keep living the life you're living. But you can't complain about your situation and hope for something different at the same time. You have to live a life of intentionality. Don't say "later" or "tomorrow"; don't flip to the next page of this book! You may not find the answer today, but you can take the first step here and now: *What is your passion? What are you visualizing?* It's not about the product. It's not about the business. It's about what you have on your mind. *Does it excite you? Do you daydream about it? Does it keep you up at night?* Don't wait for inspiration. Don't wait for your opportunity.

There is a simple formula I have lived by for decades that has been important for me to understand how people achieve results:

REBEL LEADERSHIP

Success = Passion + Discipline

When you find your passion, lock in and chase it. Every time you do something, throw yourself completely into it. Focus on one thing instead of chasing fifty little things. That's been part of my success. No matter how passionate you are, discipline is as important as any other thing. Discipline propels you to do what is right even if you don't feel like doing it. I have said this often: if you want to have success in life, you have to do things you like and things you don't like. When you don't have the discipline that you need, you're not going to get the results you want. Being disciplined in everything you do, in everything you say, and during the entire journey that you walk is critical for you to achieve your goals. You have to be able to say to yourself, *This is my path and I'm not going to deviate from it. This is what I'm going to do every day and nobody's going to move me off this path. This is my strategy, and nothing is going to throw me off course.* Discipline is the key to making everything happen. You might be capable, but without discipline you won't reach the finish line. You might be knowledgeable, but if you don't have discipline, you're not going to make it.

As I sat on the patio at Nora and Alfonso's home all those weekends learning the business, and as my team began to grow, I realized direct sales was my passion. I

PASSION AND DISCIPLINE: BECOMING #1

saw not only what it could do for me but how it affected the team I was beginning to build in Maracaibo. It consumed my every hour — day and night. It helped me keep knocking on doors when they slammed shut in my face.

BECOMING #1

It was a warm Thursday in March 1985 as I waited nervously for Nora and Alfonso to arrive at my house in Maracaibo where I was meeting with my team to share the exciting news.

After five months or so meeting up at Nora and Alfonso's home, we were beginning to compete with the best, not only in Maracaibo but in all of Venezuela. I knew Nora and Alfonso were beginning to take me seriously when they stopped asking me to buy cigarettes and beer because they recognized that I was becoming a leader and moving up within the ranks of the business. By the beginning of 1985, less than two and a half years after entering the Tupperware business and at the age of twenty-three, I received a call from the GM of Tupperware in Venezuela. Although I had found success as a sales leader in Maracaibo, Nora and Alfonso were the city's distributors at that time. The GM had noticed our success and presented us with the opportunity to become the

REBEL LEADERSHIP

Tupperware distributor in a small city named Barinas in the state of Portuguesa, very far from Maracaibo. But because Barinas was a small city, the opportunity was limited. "If you were my son," the CEO told me, "I would tell you not to accept it." Still, making the jump from sales rep to distributor was a promotion; even though the opportunity was limited, I didn't care. I was enthusiastic about the chance to move up. "Wherever you send me, I'll go," I told him. We prepared a plan and set a date for the move to Barinas. During the last week in Maracaibo with my team, the plan had been to announce, alongside Nora and Alfonso, that I would be moving to a new city. When Alfonso arrived in the middle of my team meeting, he asked if he could meet with me privately. We found a room. "Your distribution center has been canceled," he said. I threw myself onto the sofa, tears rolling down my face. The GM of Venezuela had been fired and the new GM didn't agree with our nomination, thinking it was too big of a responsibility for a twenty-three-year-old. I had already told some of my team members that I had been nominated. If I hadn't been convinced that this was the opportunity to change my quality of life, I probably would have left Tupperware. I felt I had been mocked and cheated on. Nevertheless, I wiped the tears from my face and returned to the meeting. Having to break the news to my team that my nomination had been canceled and

PASSION AND DISCIPLINE: BECOMING #1

I was not being promoted was one of the most difficult moments of my business career.

The next week, the newly named Venezuela CEO, Orlando Aguirre, arrived in Maracaibo to meet with us. He told my then-wife and I everything we'd already heard — that we were too young and that he didn't think it was right for us to take on such a great responsibility. At the end of the meeting, he asked us what we were thinking. I told him the Barinas distributorship was an opportunity for financial freedom and we were not going to quit. "And there's something important I want you to know," I told him. I'll never forget it. "Yes, we are young. But we're going to show you that we are ready and that we are mature enough to receive this type of opportunity," I said. "We're going to have the convention in July, and I know that we're going to go up there to be recognized, and each time I am recognized, I'm going to hug you and I'm going to tell you I'm ready to be given a greater opportunity."

That July we went to the convention and received a number of honors. Rosibel and Hugo were #1 at the national level, but we were #2. The top ten distributors were rewarded with a trip to Puerto Rico in late September. Orlando greeted us at the Caracas airport to say goodbye, and when we returned, he and the entire Tupperware staff waited for us at a Caracas hotel for a special dinner reception. At the end of dinner, Orlando stood up and said he had an important announcement. "Among the ten of you who are here," he said, "there is one new distributor." It was us. Only six months earlier, he didn't feel my wife and I were mature enough to be distributors. But we put in so much effort that he realized he had made a mistake by not giving us the opportunity earlier. We hadn't let adversity defeat us. We maintained our conviction. I was still twenty-three years old, the same age as I was when Orlando said I wasn't ready for the opportunity in Barinas. That was a magical night. I hugged Orlando and told him I appreciated his trust. That was the final announcement. The night was over. I left the room and began walking down the hallway. It was more than three decades ago, but I'll never forget the moment when it hit me. I stopped. *Hey*, I thought, *he didn't say where I'm going to be the distributor*. I turned around and returned to the room.

"Orlando, where is that distribution center located?" I asked.

"The people that you're going to replace have already been told that you're going to replace them," he said.

"Who are they?" I asked.

"Your bosses," Orlando said flatly.

I was stunned. The people who had taught me

PASSION AND DISCIPLINE: BECOMING #1

and guided me, who had promoted me to become a distributor — my own leaders. I would replace Nora and Alfonso. Of course, I was excited. This was a great opportunity in my own city, a big city, and one of the largest distribution centers in the entire country. But I was going to replace my very own mentors. On one hand it was beautiful, and on the other hand, it was extremely painful. When we arrived at the Maracaibo airport from Caracas, Nora and Alfonso were there to welcome us. Nora and Alfonso handled the situation with class and humility. They hugged my wife and I and said they were happy for us. Afterward, they joined us on my parents' small patio with our leaders and peers to celebrate our nomination. They were so brave. They weren't happy about what was happening, but we had become such great friends that they had the grace to accompany us and celebrate with us. Not long after they returned to their home in Valencia, Venezuela. We remained friends, but things were never the same between us.

Back in Maracaibo, I embraced my new opportunity and began the process of finding sales representatives who would help build my distribution center. One of the things I learned was that to win people over, you need to help them achieve what you're offering them. It's only then that you can ask them to do what you want them to do. During that time, I discovered that leaders still have a lot to learn, such as integrity, justice, and respect. Above all, a leader needs to be honest. Sometimes leaders have to put a pretty face on the tough messages that need to be delivered. Some people in leadership positions try to make people like them by telling them what they want to hear, even if there's no truth in it, or offer big promises where none exist. When I became the Tupperware distributor in Maracaibo, I faced a difficult situation. Being named the leader of the distribution center in Maracaibo, in the city where I was born, had never been my dream. I couldn't have dreamed it. Although I dreamed of being a distributor, I never thought it would happen for me in my hometown. What made the situation challenging was that the peers I had worked alongside for three years under Nora and Alfonso now worked under me. I had to face the fact that I was no longer going to be their partner in the business, I was going to be leading it. To further complicate the situation, all twenty-eight sales leaders in my Maracaibo distribution center were older than me. Most of them were in their forties and fifties. I was just turning twenty-three.

    One of the reasons I took over the Maracaibo distribution center was because it had become disorganized. In Tupperware's business model, distributors sold the products to sales representatives on credit. The problem in Maracaibo was that many of the leaders weren't collecting

PASSION AND DISCIPLINE: BECOMING #1

payments on time. There were no control measures in place for payments. When a business loses control over payments, it can't reach its goals. During a meeting at my house, I told the team that it was obvious there was a serious problem. "We're going to start paying by the established and required terms that the company tells us," I told the group. There was no negotiation. During the next meeting, I faced backlash. Of the twenty-eight sales leaders, fourteen either didn't understand or accept what I said had to be done. I listened to their concerns and worked with them, but I made it clear. "The only thing that is not negotiable is paying on time," I said. "Whoever doesn't do that is out of the business." I had no doubt that was what I had to correct if I wanted to have a healthy, successful business. These fourteen sales leaders had a high volume of sales in the business, and they felt powerful. They didn't accept the new condition, let alone coming from a twenty-three-year-old. I gave them some time and tried to make them understand the importance of the changes that needed to be made. I worked with them for six months, but each day became more difficult to manage. Finally, I decided enough was enough. Six months after taking over the Maracaibo distribution center, I fired fourteen of my twenty-eight sales leaders. Almost immediately there was commotion in Tupperware Venezuela. It didn't take long for Orlando, my boss, to call me.

REBEL LEADERSHIP

"I gave you this business to improve it," he said, "not to destroy it." That was a transcendent moment in my career. Orlando criticized and condemned what I had done and made it clear he didn't want me to destroy his distribution. "Are you going to reconsider your decision?" he asked.

"No," I told him, standing strong on my decision. "I'm not reconsidering." That was when I began demonstrating the character I needed as a leader. The greatest affirmation a leader has is the moment he or she is convinced a decision is correct, and I knew I'd made the right call. "You put me here to be able to make the business better, and I thought those people were rotten apples," I told Orlando. "If you put me in this position, I think I deserve the trust to make the decisions I consider appropriate."

"I'm giving you six months," he told me. "If in six months there's no improvement, you're out of the company. You can fire them, but you have to agree that if in six months the situation hasn't improved, you're giving me back the distribution center."

Those events taught me a valuable lesson: you have to be afraid of fear controlling you. You can't be afraid of being afraid because being frightened of some things is part of human nature. Letting go half of my sales force, a group that made up more than 50 percent of my business, was risky. But I saw no other way forward. If I worked with people creating a dark cloud over the

PASSION AND DISCIPLINE: BECOMING #1

business, I wasn't going to achieve any results and my distribution center would fail. I had to tackle the fact that I was going to be afraid and permanently defeat my fear. That moment illustrates that talent alone is not enough to reach your dreams. You have to be daring, bold, and firm in your decisions. At that time, I didn't have the experience or the capability that I needed to be able to develop the responsibility they had given me as a twenty-three-year-old kid. But that twenty-three-year-old kid knew where he wanted to go and knew he had to have courage and bravery to face challenges. I knew I had to be passionate about what I was doing and knew that I needed to defend the opportunity life had given me. Standing in front of me was the chance to give a lot of people a better quality of life, including my own son. The lesson in all this is that at moments in life you have to make difficult decisions. If you don't have the courage to face them, it could very well lead to you not reaching your own success. Within six months of firing half of my team, my Maracaibo branch became one of the top three distribution centers in Venezuela.

That story reminds me of a phrase I learned in Venezuela that I still use today: *Prefiero tener controlar a un caballo desbocado, que tener que empujar a un burro*, which means, "I would rather rein in a wild horse than push a donkey."

REBEL LEADERSHIP

As a Tupperware distributor, I learned that you have to make people go the extra mile. What the majority of people really want is to work from nine in the morning until four in the afternoon. After that, it doesn't matter to them if the world ends. In the long term, that mindset doesn't take you very far. Whether it's the human being of yesterday, today, or tomorrow, I believe you will always need to guide people forward. You will always need to ask for and demand more. The majority of people will lose focus. That's why the majority of people have limitations or fail to arrive at their destination, stopping along the way or changing directions to a shorter or easier route. A minority of people are strong and disciplined and accomplish what they first set out to achieve. A good leader is someone people not only follow but are also inspired to model themselves after. That's true of the past, it is also happening today, *and* it will be true tomorrow. I prefer an aggressive, risky person to one who is weak, passive, or fearful. Those qualities will never give people opportunities to find what they want.

What I learned in those times is that you have to let people walk on their own. You can't push someone who doesn't want to be pushed, but you can guide them. This lesson taught me one of the greatest assets any leader can have: empowerment. When you empower people,

PASSION AND DISCIPLINE: BECOMING #1

you have a better chance of developing leadership than when you're trying to do all the work of the people who are under your responsibility.

Another leadership quality I learned early was the ability to listen. As I was beginning my career in direct sales, I came across a book by Don Sheehan titled *Shut Up and Sell*. The book is no longer in print but its lesson still carries: A good salesperson or a good leader is not the one who speaks the most. It's the one who listens for a way to engage with people in a way to be remembered. That book was important in my early development as a leader. It taught me that listening increases one's opportunity for power. That's because when you get to know another person, you learn what they like and you find out what they need. When we talk too much, we often don't listen. I love baseball, but if I start talking to a person about baseball, and that person is not interested, he or she will be bored. When you learn to listen to people and learn what they like and what they want, you can connect with them. Human connection is dependent on listening and hearing what a person is communicating. That connection generates power. When you learn how to listen, it gives you power, and talking too much can disconnect you from a situation. Listening is more powerful than speaking.

As I built my team in Venezuela, I developed a concept that if I named a new distributor, and if I inspired them to be a distributor like I was, many more would get inspired. I was making my sales team members compete with each other. I knew each of their goals, but I challenged them to chase the team goals. As someone showed qualities of becoming a distributor, I would tell them, "You're #7. You have six people in front of you. Help me push them." Then I would tell the person in fifth, "You're #5. You have four people in front of you. You need to help me push them." I knew this would help me build a team. When I named these people as distributors, even though I knew I would lose the benefit and sales they were generating me, I knew I was going to inspire other people. What I lost on one side, I gained from the inspiration of other people. I practiced that permanently, allowing my team to rise to the top in Venezuela and creating eleven new distributors along the way to the top.

GOING BACKWARD TO GO FORWARD

By 1995, I had become a successful Tupperware distributor, ranking among the top three distributors every year for more than a decade. Still, I wasn't content with the status quo I could maintain in Maracaibo. I don't know if I recognized it consciously, but I was beginning to think about my next movie. It was a valuable lesson: after we have success it's important not to settle; it's important to

PASSION AND DISCIPLINE: BECOMING #1

look inward and say to ourselves, *Let's go for more!* I still tell people today, "Never let that hunger end." That's the key to success. If your hunger goes away, then so does your passion.

I picked up the phone and called Orlando. "I want to be part of the staff," I told him. "I don't want to be a distributor anymore." Why would I leave something so comfortable to work inside the Tupperware corporate office? I can't quite explain the feeling, but it was clear to me that it was a step I needed to take. Tupperware was not my destination. Sure, it had made me a millionaire and I could continue to go through the motions and reap the rewards. But to reach my great dream of being an independent entrepreneur without a boss, without a schedule, without someone giving me a sales target and putting a ceiling on my compensation or rewards for my effort, work, and dedication, I had no choice but to take the risk.

"You're crazy," Orlando said from the other end of the phone. "You're earning so much money as a distributor. I'm going to pay you 30 percent of what you're earning now." Orlando was right. I had earned a lot of money and was financially secure. But you can't wait for opportunities. People who wait for their big break usually find themselves sitting in the same place the next day, the next week, and the next year. I couldn't fall back on

REBEL LEADERSHIP

my success of yesterday or depend on tomorrow. I had to focus on today. It's impossible to chase your dream without sacrifice. Sometimes you have to give up something good for the opportunity of something better. Tomorrow's success starts today. And today, I was ready to give up my comfort for the potential of the unknown. "I don't care what you pay me," I told Orlando. "I want to learn what corporate life is like. I want you to give me the opportunity of being there and seeing how to manage this, because one day I want to be the owner of my own company." Orlando didn't accept my offer.

As the next week wore on, I couldn't stand the *what-if* thoughts and the possibility of regret that consumed me. So many people say "tomorrow" only to find themselves in their thirties, forties, fifties, and sixties saying, "if only." I decided to call Orlando back. "Here's your distribution center," I told him. "I don't want it anymore." Walking away was a risky proposition, but I knew if I applied pressure, he might accept my offer. Sure enough, Orlando offered me the position of sales director of the entire western region of Venezuela.

When I arrived at the corporate office, I asked Orlando to please invite me to any meeting I could be a part of. I wanted to know about finance, marketing, human resources. I didn't have much knowledge about the corporate side of direct sales, but I had learned a lot

PASSION AND DISCIPLINE: BECOMING #1

from running my own distribution center. I knew how to control inventory, how to control finances, and how to manage a staff of fifteen or twenty people, but this was something totally different. This was a corporation with global management, spread across not just Venezuela but the entire world. That's what I wanted to learn, and that's why I took the risk. I had the dream of creating and building my own company, and that desire led me to a job that offered less money but provided an opportunity to earn in knowledge what it lacked in pay.

Shortly after I moved to the corporate side of Tupperware, I met a woman named Marjorie Munoz who would later join me on the leadership team at Tupperware. It was Marjorie's first job, and after a few weeks working together, she was amazed to find out I had come from being the #1 distributor in Venezuela, with big earnings, to being an employee of the company. She didn't understand how I could turn away from a career worth millions. I explained that to build my own company I needed the knowledge and experience the new position offered. She wasn't convinced. A few years later, when I called Marjorie to join my new company, it finally hit her. She understood my intention of going from a successful career with guarantees to one with no guarantee of advancement in order to gain knowledge that would have an impact on my future. It was a measured

REBEL LEADERSHIP

risk with vision and offered a valuable lesson. Sometimes you have to go backward to go forward.

The problem so many people face is they think success is a destination. Success doesn't come with crossing a proverbial finish line — that big promotion, that award, that financial milestone — it comes along the journey to that dream. Success comes from dreaming big, sacrificing what you have today for opportunity tomorrow, and committing to intentional growth. Don't stop growing. Don't become complacent. You can be the most passionate person in the universe, but passion without discipline is useless. If you're not brave enough to step into the unknown and daring enough to make it happen, you are never going to reach the opportunities that life could give you.

Nothing in life is free. Making the decision to join the corporate staff and leave behind my freedom as an independent entrepreneur cost me a lot of money, but it was a necessary price to pay. So without hesitating, I set out on the road to a better tomorrow. I know that you have had or will have to do things that you don't like or that are not economically convenient for you, but if those decisions or challenges are on the path of your dreams, do not hesitate to take the path now. Do not waste time. Don't put things off until tomorrow. The destination is worth the price.

CHAPTER 6

HITTING ROCK BOTTOM

I STARED at the television across the living room in disbelief as my sixth and final bet of the day turned up a loser. That Sunday morning, I had placed six sports bets at the gambling room in Maracaibo, and now my fate was settled. I had come up a loser.

0-for-6. Zilch. *Nada.*

Earlier that morning, I had made a promise to Leudin. I was going to place bets on the six games I usually did on Sundays and then pray to God and ask for the strength to lose on all six games. "Once I lose all six games," I told Leudin, "I'm going to understand that God is talking to me to give me a message that gambling is not the correct path." That night, I heard God's message loud and clear. Out of the six games I bet and lost that day, two were absolute stunners. Earlier in the day, the

REBEL LEADERSHIP

baseball team I bet on led by a score of 8-0 in the eighth inning, only to lose in extra innings. My sixth and final bet of the day was the National Football League game, and my team was up by two points with just ten seconds remaining. The quarterback took the snap, and instead of falling on the ball to run down the clock, he fumbled the ball, and the defense recovered and scored a touchdown to win. I had lost $60,000. Since then, I have kept the promise I made to Leudin and myself. I have never bet on sports again. Of course, at that time, I had no choice. I was broke.

What led me on the path toward that fateful day was my decision to leave the Tupperware business in 1995. After spending more than a year in the Tupperware Venezuela corporate office learning everything I could, Orlando was fired as general manager and replaced. The new general manager asked me to stay on for a few more months to help build a connection between the factory and the distributors in Venezuela, but I wasn't happy that the company had fired my boss, my leader, the one who had given me all the opportunities to grow in direct sales. I planned to leave, but I decided to make a crazy demand in exchange for staying on for three more months. I thought he would say no, but to my surprise he agreed. That was the beginning of the end of my experience in Tupperware. I had a feeling at that time that my life in direct sales was

HITTING ROCK BOTTOM

coming to an end, and after three months, I searched for other opportunities outside the industry.

My first project outside of direct sales was in an area completely unknown to me. Along with my brothers, I partnered on a construction project for a residential building in my home state of Zulia. My first experience wasn't so bad. I was willing to try different occupations where the money was good.

One day, as I sat in a friend's gambling room in Maracaibo watching sports on TV, he told me how good gambling could be. I dared to do it myself. I purchased my first lottery ticket when I was sixteen years old but had only recently begun sports betting in my thirties. On weekends, I began to dedicate my days, from 1 p.m. until 12 a.m., watching sports and betting on games. I started betting on horse races, baseball, basketball, American football — whatever was on the TV screen. I bet on *everything*. Listening to my friend and seeing with my own eyes how many sports bettors were there, glued to the screens, I decided then and there that I should open my own gambling room. *It's going to be one of the best in the city*, I thought. Along with my brother Leonardo, I purchased a rundown, hole-in-the-wall restaurant building in the city and completely renovated it. The building had been in precarious condition when we bought it, but we invested in it to make it luxurious. TVs lined the place so people could see whatever games they wanted to watch. The small, uncomfortable chairs were replaced with relaxing armchairs. I'll never forget how it looked. It became the most beautiful gambling room in all of Maracaibo, and by the end of 1996, Tio Cheo was open for sports bets. The business grew very big, very quickly and we started earning a lot of money. Many weeks, our profits would total $150,000. That's more than $275,000 in American dollars today, and it was an especially large amount of money in Venezuela in the 1990s.

I poured my energy into Tio Cheo. Each day I would watch what was happening in Las Vegas and at other gambling rooms and set the betting lines. People could place bets on televised games. I would sell the tickets with a commission and finance the bets with my own personal bank account. When I didn't like the bets, I passed them to another betting house and charged a commission. My mother worked for free managing the kitchen, and of course she came up with incredible meals that everybody liked and that kept people hanging around longer, giving them time to place more bets. The person I hired as the cook, William Acurero, stayed with me and remains my personal chef to this day. He is like a brother to me now. Tio Cheo became one of the top gambling rooms in the city, at least until I started believing I could start placing sports bets myself

HITTING ROCK BOTTOM

to earn even more money than I already was earning. That was my great mistake. That's what ruined me. I started dreaming that I would open more businesses that would be as successful as the gambling room and that I would be a great entrepreneur. I made a daring move when I started betting myself, and then everything came crashing down. My mistake wasn't starting Tio Cheo; the business was a great success. My failure came when I left my discipline behind and lost my focus.

It was ironic that my first success came from carrying pink bags and my second success was a macho gambling room offering sports betting. It was like going from one extreme to the other. Those two situations taught me a lot. I had a very good business that stopped being a good business when I started gambling. What hit me hardest was that *my success was at the expense and ruin of others*. I made money, but the consequence of me winning was that other people lost their money. It was sad to see those people leaving the gambling room with bitter faces. Sometimes they would bet their entire week's salary. Knowing I had won didn't make me feel good. I realized to be successful like I was in Tupperware I needed to make other people successful too. I knew I was on the wrong path. I always knew that. But I became conscious of it when I watched the last $60,000 I had to my name crumble.

I didn't have any money. Leudin and I were hiding in our apartment to avoid paying rent. The day I locked the doors of Tio Cheo, I reassured Ray. "I'm sure that I will do fine," I told him. "You're going to see that it's going to be even better." The truth was, my car sat empty along the street. I didn't even have enough money for gas.

A BLESSING AMID MY MISTAKES

Nobody sets out in life to fail. In fact, many people don't reach their full potential because they are afraid to fail. The failures in my life have taught me an important lesson. My failures haven't come because I didn't take chances but because I lost focus on what was important—my True North. I was daring, but I forgot to bring my discipline along on the journey with me.

It was only in my failures that I learned a valuable lesson: respect success, respect power, and respect money. Because when you don't respect these three things, what took you to the top can take you to rock bottom.

When someone starts becoming successful, it's easy to start feeling powerful. The more success you have, the more powerful you feel. You think that money will never end, that success will never end, and that you know everything there is to know. That was a hard

HITTING ROCK BOTTOM

reflection to stumble on. I had to live in a situation like the one I lived to be able to understand it. It's important to remember that we are human and that we have achieved many goals, but we have made mistakes along the way. To be able to heal those wounds we must understand, accept, and reflect on our errors.

I'm not perfect. Throughout my life I've done inappropriate things that affected my children's and my family's happiness, and I know it caused a lot of frustration along the way. I'm human. Before I met Leudin, I didn't always make the best decisions for my children and family. I wasn't loyal. I wasn't making the right choices. Eventually, I realized I needed to reflect on my errors to begin healing the wounds they caused, which probably would never heal completely. In the moment, it was difficult to see my mistakes and poor behavior, but I realized I needed to see what I had done in order to heal and move forward.

Thankfully, Leudin entered my life at just the right moment, just as Tio Cheo was beginning to find success. Every Monday I would take the stack of checks to the bank across Maracaibo. I'll never forget the day I spotted Leudin across the bank cashing checks with her father. She was beautiful. Through my weekly trips to deposit Tio Cheo's earnings, I had come to know the bank manager. I decided to ask him for a favor. "The next

REBEL LEADERSHIP

time that girl comes into the bank, call me," I told him. "Tell them the check has a problem, tell them whatever you want, but keep them in the bank. I'll come within the hour." It wasn't long after that my phone rang. "Luis, I'm gonna tell them that there is something wrong with the check," the manager told me. "But you better hurry." Within fifteen minutes, I was at the bank. She was outside the waiting area with her dad, so I went to the manager's office and asked him to call her in while her dad waited in the lobby. When Leudin walked in, I told her nothing was wrong with the check. "But I want to get to know you," I said. "Could we have dinner?" She was quiet and shy. I gave her my business card. About a month later I was reading the local newspaper when I saw an article. There was Leudin, the winner of the beauty pageant. *Oh my god*, I thought, *this is the girl from the bank*. She never called! I knew what I was going to do. I asked the bank manager for her address and went to the florist. "Give me the biggest one you have," I told her. "I want the biggest possible arrangement you can ever do." I put my number inside, Leudin called, and the rest is history.

Leudin was the blessing I needed in my life. Because while I had promised to make better decisions in my relationships, when I went into the gambling business, it damaged years of opportunity. It was another moment when I deviated from my appropriate behavior to achieve

HITTING ROCK BOTTOM

my goals. Leudin is fifteen years younger than me, and people — even family members — always talked about how she married me for money. When I met Leudin, even though I became loyal to her and I became a better person, the process of righting my path didn't happen overnight. I was still making big decisions that were bad decisions, to the point where I lost everything gambling. When I went bankrupt in 1998 and Leudin stood by my side, it forced everyone into silence. She stayed with me in my weakest moment. We went through years of crisis, but we came out of the crisis together.

LOOKING IN THE MIRROR

With each passing day at Tio Cheo, as I placed bet after bet — first to earn more income and then to dig myself out of the hole of crushing debt I had dug — I was deteriorating. It's a funny thing that I never realized until it was over. If you hang out with rotten tomatoes, you're going to become a rotten tomato yourself.

Through my rise in direct sales I always told people, "You need to show up dressed sharp. Like a winner, always." The people who sat at Tio Cheo day and night became disheveled and sloppy, me included. I wore any shirt I could find and stopped combing my hair. There is a saying in Spanish, *El que anda con cojos, al final*

REBEL LEADERSHIP

cojea, that loosely translates to, "The one that hangs out with those who limp, ends up limping." I was disheveled and dejected. Through all my success-filled years, my image was everything to me. I had worn colorful suits and dressed for success. People talked about my appearance. "What happened to your father?" people would ask my children. I looked at myself in the mirror. I was a disaster.

There are moments in life, as we head down the wrong path, that we are suddenly snapped back to reality. As I began to gamble away our bank account, eventually relying on friends to lend me money to feed the addiction, the same thing was happening to the people around me before my very eyes. I remember one day, having lost everything, a friend begged for the chance to place another bet in hopes that it would be the big winner. With no money to bet with, he made me a proposal. He owned some houses and properties. He would put them in my name, giving the properties as a guarantee, so I could loan him the money. I knew him, so I accepted the offer. With time, the dates arrived to repay his loan, but he didn't have the money. He lost the properties, including his own house. With nowhere to live, he returned to Tio Cheo and told me he was broke. I gave him an extension, but he wasn't able to pay. The properties were transferred to my

HITTING ROCK BOTTOM

name. Four months after the deadline passed, the guy showed back up. "I have the money to pay," he told me through tears. "I know the deadline has already passed, but can you consider giving me back my properties?" Though accepting the proposal would cost me money — the properties were worth much more than I had lent him — I went back to an important lesson my mom and dad taught me that I always take into consideration: always do the right thing and always be fair. Leudin and I were headed toward a crisis, and I knew we could use the money. But we also knew it wasn't right to take the man's properties. We weren't going to earn the amount of money we would have with those properties, which might have given us a few more months to pay our rent and debts, but we would be at peace because we had done the right thing. We gave the man his properties back.

That was my moment of revelation. These people gambled their week's paycheck, their savings, their families' homes. *Oh, my god*, I thought, *I'm the avenue*. Sure, the reason for their poor behavior was their gambling addictions, but I was the one who created the opportunity for them to lose everything. When you're inside that world you don't know how to get out. You don't see bad things as you're living through them. What started out being an enormous business opportunity for us became hell. I didn't know how to escape that pit until I was completely ruined. I asked myself, *Am I going to be someone who's going to enable people to lose money, or am I going to be someone who helps people make money and changes the quality of their life?*

Betting had become a habit and a necessity. I saw all my money disappearing but I kept going, betting more in hopes of recovering my money. Instead of being something positive, it was becoming more negative day after day. Watching that man lose everything broke me, but I'll be honest, I stopped because gambling ruined *me.* I had nothing left. When I lost that final bet and my $60,000 vanished, I was done.

As the interest payments stacked up on the gambling room, Leonardo and I had no choice but to sell. It was enough to pay a small part of what I owed to the creditor. Bankruptcy helped with the rest. When Leonardo and I sold Tio Cheo, we didn't even have enough to eat. Just as we owed people money, there were people who owed us money from unpaid bets. I couldn't do anything but wait for payments to come in. I remember $100 coming in one week. "Here, Leonardo," I said, "$50 for you and $50 for me." The next week Leonardo collected $200. "$100 for you, $100 for me," he said. It was hardly enough to survive. I took Leudin's jewelry to the pawn shop, we hid from the landlords,

HITTING ROCK BOTTOM

and I searched for new horizons. It was a dark and hard moment, but those difficult moments never took away the faith and the hope of fighting for our best opportunities. I think that was crucial. I started working with a lot of dedication and focus. I wasn't afraid.

When you're able to educate yourself to be able to face difficult situations, you can accomplish the results you deserve, especially when you learn from your failures. I went down the wrong path and caused my business to fail. The risk was appropriate, but the way I managed my behavior and used my money was wrong. I lost my focus. Of all the experiences I've been through, I've learned many things along the way. I've learned that to mature you have to be brave, you have to dominate your fears, and you have to be aware of your strengths and your weaknesses. I always tell my kids, and I'll repeat it: respect money, respect success, respect power. Because if you let money dominate you, if you let success dominate you, and if you let power dominate you, you're on the way to failure.

Cleaning up my image for my family's sake inspired me in those dark moments, and it still inspires me today. Being ruined and having to leave that world by force brought me back to direct sales. Thank God I'm here. When I was in Tupperware, I needed to help other people attain success to have success myself. At Tio

Cheo, for me to win, another person had to lose, and that went against my beliefs. It made me realize that I had to go back to direct sales because, in order for me to win, I needed to make other people win as well. I knew what I needed to do.

CHAPTER 7

STARTING FROM ZERO

I SCANNED the closet in our apartment the morning of my interview at the local coffee shop in Caracas, hoping to find something, anything, that would present a better image than the one that was circulating in direct sales circles in Venezuela. Just as my opportunities in business had vanished, my once-abundant wardrobe had shrunk as well. On a hanger was one last suit, a green Christian Dior design that had matching olive green dress shoes. Ironically, even that was damaged. What was once a masterpiece now had a hole right in the back. I had no choice. I slipped on the jacket and headed out the door to chase a new beginning.

The day I stared out the living room window, tears streaming down my face, promising Leudin that we would be successful again, I had no doubt what my next move had to be. I had to go back to direct sales. I didn't know anything else, and it was my passion. Just as I had done nearly twenty years earlier, I knocked on doors. Although I had spent four years outside of Tupperware, I had gone out on top. I had been the #1 distributor in all of Venezuela. I was certain people would welcome me. I realized then that when you have money, friends are everywhere, but when you are at your lowest, you find out who your true friends are. I felt like I was back on Plaza Baralt begging people to watch my product demonstrations. People looked down on me and slammed doors in my face. They said I was a gambler, that my image was ruined, that I was obsolete. If there is one thing that can dash a person's spirits, it's having to start from scratch, either because the foundation wasn't good enough or because of being forced to change direction. Dejected, I felt as if I had no path back. I didn't have anything or anybody and needed to find a way to survive.

One evening, I told Leudin about a young man named Alex Juarez, whom I introduced to Tupperware and coached through success with the company. Alex had left Tupperware and joined a direct-sales company called SwissJust that sold essential oils and body lotions. At that time, it wasn't a large company, but it was a stable business and Alex had become general manager. I was out of options. I picked up the phone and called. "Alex, I

STARTING FROM ZERO

don't have a job. I'm ruined. I don't have anything to do," I confessed. "Tupperware closed its doors to me. Can you give me a job?" Alex was open and confided in me that people told him he was crazy for considering me for a position and that my image was tarnished from gambling. He said that others told him I would come in and displace him. Thankfully, his memory of me was one of success. Alex decided he needed someone like me on his team, but the decision wasn't completely up to him. The owner of the company wanted to meet me first. That's why I put on my old Christian Dior suit. Fortunately, the owner didn't have any preconceived notions about me. I did the interview, and the owner gave Alex authorization to make the call. Because of our friendship, he offered me the opportunity to become a regional manager. The position came with a very low salary, but it didn't matter. This was my chance to get back into direct sales, an open door that I felt would lead to a better path. "I have to accept this offer," I told Leudin. "It's the only way that I'm going to be able to go back." Thanks to Alex Juarez, I'm in direct sales to this day. Nobody else opened the door. If not for Alex, maybe I wouldn't be in direct sales. If not for Alex, maybe MONAT would still be just a dream.

I don't know a single person who is successful that hasn't had failure in their life. For many years, people have asked me the reason for my failure after having

REBEL LEADERSHIP

achieved in such a short period of time what was impossible for many. How did I go from being a millionaire in my twenties to ruined at thirty-nine? The answer has always eluded me, but after analyzing it, I realized I'd lost sight of a great truth: you can't stray from your True North. Whether your life is filled with success or you find doors slamming in your face, you have to keep focus on the path straight ahead and take care to avoid temptations and diversions along the way. You have to maintain your True North and have the strength to face the difficult moments that stand in the way. The path to success does not travel in a straight line. There will be potholes — some deeper than others — that slow you down or throw you off track. You can't avoid them all as you make your way through life, but you can control how you respond.

After being admired by so many people, I needed courage and strength to start again from zero. I didn't care what people said; I didn't allow my ego to dominate me. I left that aside. I knew who I was, and I was convinced that I was able to succeed. Starting all over again and going from house to house — something I thought I had left in the past — was difficult, but I knew I had to do it. Enjoy your successes — don't live life in fear of failure — but understand that at any point, you can fail, and that even when you fail, if your willingness is big enough, you can come out of it. I lived that. I started

STARTING FROM ZERO

knocking on doors again. I started attending home meetings again. I started to develop new leaders. After having everything, I started from zero.

There is a saying I remember: "It is no disgrace to start all over. It is usually an opportunity."

SUCCESS AND SUFFERING

It's no coincidence that *success* and *suffering* are close to each other in the dictionary. They go hand in hand. There is no way to attain success without suffering.

Success doesn't come easy. When I started in direct sales and I was knocking on doors holding two pink bags, holding demonstrations on the plaza, it was tough. When I started again, traveling from city to city with no money, nobody would have known if I'd just given up.

Ever since the day Alex said *yes*, Leudin and I worked from morning to night because I knew that was the only way I was going to be able to overcome the current situation. In the morning, we'd travel six hours across Venezuela to another city, where we'd knock on doors to show the products. Whenever possible, we'd find a run-down, cheap hotel to stay the night. Many days, with no options, we hit the road and spent the night driving home. Some days we were on the road for twelve hours. On many occasions, the trips resulted in zero sales. Understanding that I had to persevere to achieve results and that I would encounter more negative results than favorable ones reinforced a valuable lesson. I had to keep knocking on doors, on the good days and bad, to achieve success. Many people don't want to face the truth. Most people want an easy business or an easy life and they surrender too quickly, too easily. There is no way of succeeding without suffering or sacrificing. Sometimes sacrifice is so painful that it makes a person lose focus, and they lose the will to live, but once a person gets past it and can see the bigger picture of how the pain led to the end goal, it's easier to understand. Everybody wants to live a beautiful life, without sacrifice and without suffering. It doesn't exist. If I hadn't accepted that challenge and I hadn't sacrificed or suffered through so much, I wouldn't be here today, right here, right now. Success is achieved by effort, a lot of fight, believing in your dreams, and a lot of suffering.

Suffering doesn't always come as one big awakening, and it isn't always dire. People often think of suffering as losing a job, receiving a bad health diagnosis, or some other traumatic life event. The truth is, many times suffering comes in the form of daily struggles that accompany us as we chase our goals and dreams. We encounter suffering when we step out into the unknown and face our fears in hope of a better tomorrow. Suffering is the pain we face, the daily sacrifices we make, and the price we pay in pursuit of our passion. Suffering is being comfortable with being uncomfortable.

Suffering, in my estimation, can come in many forms.

1. Pain and Sacrifice

You've probably heard the saying, "If it were easy, everyone would be doing it." Nothing worthwhile comes easy. You can choose the path of a nine-to-five job, with a comfortable income and a comfortable life. There is nothing wrong with that. Many people choose that path. But living a life without regret means paying the price now for enjoyment later. Think about it: *Are you truly doing what you love? Are you living the life you want?* There will be trade-offs along the journey, but you have to be willing to pay the price. During my early days in direct sales, there were many times I had to leave my son at his grandmother's house while we traveled. My family and friends criticized us for doing that. My reply was always firm. "I'm going to sacrifice being present with my son today, so I can give my son the satisfaction of tomorrow." It's ironic, right? Family was my sole driving force to get out of my situation, and I left them behind? It was a sacrifice I had to make — for me *and* them. That didn't mean forever, but for a year or two, it was the price I had to pay. Today, I have the satisfaction of seeing my children empowered, with strong positive habits and the ability to thrive with the legacy that I helped create after so many years of effort. I always remind them that to be where we are now, we had to work hard. It was painful then, but now I am satisfied. I achieved success.

2. Doubters and Naysayers
Negativity and darkness (what I call "dark clouds") move all around us during the pursuit of our passions. Any life worth living can't just be rainbows and sunshine. Dark clouds present themselves in different ways as we make our way through life. There are doubters and critics and naysayers, and while all of these people present different challenges on the way to our goals, they all bring negativity to our journey and act as dream-killers if we allow them to. Doubters lack faith in our pursuits and question our dreams; critics tear apart our work; naysayers fill our lives with negativity with a constant lack of belief. Success depends on having conviction and strength in your decisions every day. Don't let anyone steal your dreams. You always have to search for a "why" to inspire you, especially when you're mired in difficult times.

I was told that Tupperware was a women's business; when I was twenty-three people said I was too young to be a distributor; I was told I was crazy when I fired half of my sales force; people said I was washed up. Sometimes their words hurt. Sometimes doubt crept in, but I knew I had to have conviction in my decisions. When I started on my way as a leader in direct sales, I said I wanted to be rich. Many people, including family members, told me that there wasn't room for more rich people, and yet I reaffirmed my intention to be rich. "They are not full because I am not there," I said. "At some point in time one of them will die because of old age, and I will enter."

3. Fear and Failure

Sometimes, in order to be successful, when your legs start shaking, you have to keep them under the table. You can't allow fear to dominate you. If fear dominates you, it will lead you down the wrong path. That's why I always say, whether it ends up being right or wrong, you have to dare to make decisions. When you feel empowered, only then will you start living the type of situations that will destroy fear. "But what if I fail?" people ask. That's OK. Go ahead, try it, and if you fail, dare to do it again. Many people see leaders and successful men and women as people who are perpetually happy and who face no adversity. That's not true. People who have achieved success are the people who have encountered adversities and challenges permanently. Let me show you some examples that transcend culture.

REBEL LEADERSHIP

- When he was in his twenties, Walt Disney was fired from his newspaper job and told by his editor that he "lacked imagination and had no good ideas." Imagine saying that about the person who would help bring Mickey Mouse to life and dream up Disney World!

- Can you imagine getting fired from your own company? That's what happened to Steve Jobs. After he created Apple, Jobs was fired by his board before returning years later. Today Jobs is remembered across the world for his innovation and as the mind behind products including the Mac, iPod, and iPhone. Apple, meanwhile, became a $1 trillion company.

- Oprah Winfrey was fired as an evening news reporter because her bosses said she was too emotional and "unfit for television news." Instead, she moved to daytime television, ultimately becoming arguably the most acclaimed talk show host with a net worth of $2.5 billion.

- Twelve different publishers rejected J. K. Rowling's original manuscript before it was finally picked up. It would become known as *Harry Potter and the*

STARTING FROM ZERO

Sorcerer's Stone. In time, *Harry Potter* became a worldwide franchise that has sold more than five hundred million copies across the globe and has become a blockbuster movie collection.

- Before she became known globally by her first name, Madonna worked at Dunkin' Donuts, where she was fired within her first week for playing with the jelly and not taking the job seriously enough. Today she is known as the Queen of Pop and is the bestselling female singer of all time.

The list goes on and on. You might know those names today — they carry from America to Venezuela and across the world — but they wouldn't be well-known if they had stopped when they faced rejection or were told they weren't good enough. They all could have given up and taken an easier path and nobody would have known differently, but they refused to let fear dominate them. They got back up, over and over again.

In one of my routine readings on leadership, I came across the theory of grit, coined by a psychologist named Angela Duckworth. Grit is based on two ideas: passion and perseverance. For years, Duckworth studied the US Army, sales teams, and students to uncover what predicts whether someone will be successful. During one of her speeches on the subject, she summed it up:

One characteristic emerged as a significant predictor of success. It wasn't social intelligence, it wasn't good looks, physical health, and it wasn't IQ. It was grit. Grit is passion and perseverance for very long-term goals. Grit is having stamina. Grit is sticking with your future, day in, day out, not just for the week, not just for the month, but for years, and working really hard to make that future a reality. Grit is living life like it's a marathon, not a sprint. We have to be willing to fail, to be wrong, to start over again with lessons learned.

As I sit here now, it's satisfying and comforting to know deep inside me that passion and perseverance have been my engine to achieve the goals I set in my life. Even without this theory being present in my life through those years, not only myself but many leaders who trained me, who were my mentors, had it very clearly in their minds. To chase my passion, I had to persevere.

THE ROAD BACK TO SUCCESS

Shortly after Alex hired me to be a regional manager in Venezuela for SwissJust, he called me and the other

STARTING FROM ZERO

regional manager into his office to share our sales goals. Alex had recently returned from the United States, and after presenting the sales targets, he pulled out two watches he had bought on the trip. I am a lifelong watch lover, but at that point, I didn't have a single one because Leudin's and my jewelry were at the pawn shop.

The sales goals were aggressive, and I wasn't sure if they were achievable, but I didn't hesitate. "I accept," I told Alex. I reached out my hand and asked for the watch. "Why should I give you the watch right away?" Alex asked. "It's for when you meet the goal." I shook his hand. "I'm sure I'll make it," I said. "And if I don't, I'll pay you." Alex and I still laugh about that moment today because the truth was, I didn't have any money, and we both knew it.

When I joined SwissJust, Leudin was a quiet, timid twenty-three-year-old who had never worked, but she was adamant we work together. "Just teach me how to do it so I can help you," she said. When she started observing what I would do, she started doing it herself, and she became my most important ally who helped me keep my focus and stay disciplined. As a young woman whose husband is fifteen years her senior, Leudin still took control of situations and circumstances to support and sustain me.

To create a market, Leudin and I had no choice but to work seven days a week. We began working with a woman named Verónica Rodríguez, whom I had first met when I worked at the bank as a teenager. She was also one of my sales leaders when I had my Tupperware distribution center. In order to travel around Venezuela, we would have to get up in the still-dark hours of the morning and leave our apartment in Maracaibo. We didn't have money to pay anybody to watch our one-year-old daughter, Luisana, so Leudin or I would take her out of the crib in the middle of the night still in her pajamas, and the four of us would cram into the car and hit the road. We left so early that we didn't even have the time to feed or change Luisana before we left the apartment. Once we were on the road, Leudin would feed her, and when we stopped at gas stations on the way or between stops, Veronica would help us change her diaper. And that's how we did it, day and night, from city to city. The three adults worked together in the car, and at night I conducted the sales presentations in homes and taught Leudin the business. As we drove, I talked business with Veronica through the rearview mirror. As the days passed, we started having success again. We started growing.

It was during that time that I confirmed, once again, if you inspire someone to dream, if you can figure out what they are passionate about and you inspire them, then you will help that person find the strength to confront adversity and succeed. A team can achieve more than an individual, and it's important for a leader to have the inspiration to search for and find the True North of every person around them.

Never forget this lesson that in order to achieve success and objectives for ourselves, we first have to push for our people to achieve success. *For you to be successful, make your team successful.* That will be your best strength or your biggest weakness if you don't.

When I promised Leudin I would make it in direct sales again and rebuild my career, at some points, I thought it would be almost impossible at my age. I was thirty-nine years old when I asked myself, *Do I have a chance? Do I have the opportunity to achieve everything that I had in the past?* I had fought for twenty years to have what I once had. The negative thoughts and doubts started to dominate, but when all those questions went through my head, I didn't have a chance of doing anything else. I just had to start all over again. I decided, *No, I can start from zero*. And I was able to achieve that. At any age you are able to achieve your dreams. You have to have courage, you have to have your feet strong on the ground, and you have to make a firm decision of what to do in critical moments. The one who is a coward is the one who surrenders. The cowardly one gets tired. The coward is not inspired. They let themselves be absorbed by difficult situations. On the other hand, the people who have courage and are bold search for inspiration. In my case, my children inspired me. It took many things to have the strength to start again. I converted the negative into positive. I believed in myself, and the people who didn't believe in me didn't destroy me; they further inspired me.

One year after I started at SwissJust, our region became the most successful region in company history. Not only did we reach the goals Alex had set, but we doubled them. I hadn't made it yet, but I was back on my feet.

If you consider yourself a true leader, always remember to finish what you start. Opportunity knows neither rich nor poor, white or black, young or old. It is not a riddle, much less luck. It is simple: opportunity is for whoever takes it. Or, as my brother Leonardo used to say, "The opportunity is behind the door, and if they don't open it for me, I will knock it down. No one will stop me in pursuit of my passion and goals."

CHAPTER 8

KNOWING YOUR WORTH

I REALLY DON'T know when the best time is to start chasing your dream. It could be when you're at your best spiritually or when you're well off economically, or perhaps when the stars align. For me, it was when I was at my worst economically, without money, and in deep debt, but with passion and a deep desire to achieve my dream of having my own direct sales company. The right moment for me came in 2001, with everything working against me, but I had faith and a certainty that if I had discipline and kept my mind focused on my goal, nothing and no one would keep me from it.

When I returned to direct sales at SwissJust, I was all in. Despite being offered a salary that barely allowed Leudin and me to meet our monthly needs, I was completely dedicated. The challenge of rebuilding a direct sales business and sales force and the idea of a better opportunity tomorrow — which the owner promised — was enough to keep me focused seven days a week on the road ahead. After just a year, my work and dedication paid off; my sales territory hit the top in sales and I excitedly scheduled a meeting with Alex and the company's owner. I was certain that I was due for a big raise. At the meeting, I went over my results from the year. "Now tell me," I said, "how are you going to help me out with a raise?" Instead of giving me the raise I felt I deserved, the owner laughed, which led me to a critical decision. Instead of working for others, it was time to find a way to create my own business. That's the moment I took my first steps toward my dream. "I don't know what you're going to do with me, but I'm going to be honest with you," I told Alex after the meeting. "I'm going to start looking for something else to do. I'm going to be my own boss."

When I returned to our apartment in Maracaibo, I was still fuming. As I sat there thinking about the business, I called Ray in Miami and told him what the owner had done. "We need to start our own business," I told him. I knew I had Ray, but we needed a team. The long drives across Venezuela continued in the weeks that followed as Leudin, Veronica, and I continued on with SwissJust. One day, as Veronica sat in the back with the baby, I flipped the rearview mirror to pull her into view. "Veronica," I said, catching her eyes, "I have the business

KNOWING YOUR WORTH

of your life." Veronica was employed by SwissJust, but in a sense, she also freelanced for me as part of a sales force, helping grow the business. I had brought Veronica with me to SwissJust from Tupperware and she had become a champion, earning a trip to Mexico as a top salesperson. "I hope it's not little boxes," she said, referring to a common direct sales idea at the time predicated on little boxes with forty-something products inside. Leudin and I looked at each other and then back at Veronica. "Oh, my god," she said, "it's those little boxes!" Veronica was right, and she wasn't convinced. It was clear Veronica would take some time to convince, but I wasn't deterred from chasing the dream of my own direct sales business. Instead, I called Dubi Lugo and her husband, Jose Luis Piña, who had replaced me as distributors in Maracaibo when I left Tupperware. Soon after, Leudin and I sat with Dubi and Jose Luis in our apartment, and we still couldn't explain the whole business plan; it was a work in progress. "Come with me," I told them. They couldn't see the vision. "That doesn't sound good," they said. As the late night turned into 2 a.m. and then 3 a.m. — and the glasses of whiskey were refilled one after the next — the sales pitch continued. Dubi and Jose Luis had doubts, but by the time they left our apartment in the early morning hours, they had thought about it and decided to ride with me and Leudin and join the business.

REBEL LEADERSHIP

That morning, I called Veronica. "Come over and join me," I told her. "We're going to have a successful business here." She wouldn't believe me. I insisted that the business was almost ready, but as hard as I tried, Alex was her boss and she was committed to him. It seemed inevitable she would remain with SwissJust. Around that time Veronica took a trip to Acapulco on the western coast of Mexico. When she returned, she came to my office. "Veronica, we're ready. I'm waiting for you," I told her. My legs were shaking under the table. *This woman is going to tell me she doesn't want to work with me*, I thought. Still, I was firm. "This business is starting. With you or without you we're going to be successful," I told her. "Go ahead and make your decision." I found out later that during her trip Veronica had written a beautiful letter to me saying goodbye. Now she was in my office to tell me she was staying with Alex and SwissJust. And yet the words that came out of her mouth said otherwise. She smiled. "No, no," she said. "I'm coming to tell you *yes*." Veronica had been so moved that she changed her mind and decided to join me as a sales director. There were many stages where I didn't know what was going to happen, but faith prevailed and I trusted everything would come together.

It was October 2001 when I finally convinced Veronica, Dubi, and Jose Luis to join me and Leudin in

KNOWING YOUR WORTH

our new direct sales business. When I convinced them, I was ready. I quit SwissJust and took the leap of faith. I knew that to find people who would follow us in growing our business, the first thing we needed to do was show we were successful. The problem was, I was the only one with a vehicle, and it was an ugly red Chevrolet Cavalier with a bad engine. That made it difficult for everybody to get out and knock on doors to drum up new business. I made a promise. "In January, you will have a new car, you will have a new car, and I will have a new car," I told them. To get to that point, first we had to juggle the unreliable automobile. Each morning, I would lend my car to Veronica or Dubi, whoever arrived first. To get the engine going, we'd open both front doors of the parked car, and then two of us would push it until the engine purred and fired up. We continued like that for three months.

During the final months of 2001, we traveled across Venezuela from city to city like nomads. One day, in order to travel together to an event, we rented an old, raggedy bus. After finishing a meeting that afternoon in one city, we returned to the road at dusk en route to another city. These roads were not like the ones in the United States. They were dark and narrow, surrounded by bushes. As we made our way down the middle of the road, it was frigidly cold inside the bus. "It's really cold," we told the bus driver. "Can you lower the air conditioning, please?"

REBEL LEADERSHIP

He shouted back. "Sir, the problem is that if I have to turn off the air conditioner, I need to stop the bus and go under the bus. I cannot turn it off from the inside." That was fine by us. "Well, just go ahead and stop." We pulled off to the side of the road in the dark, the bus driver turned off the air conditioning, and we were back on our way. Ten minutes later, smoke from the engine flooded the bus. "Sir, we're choking!" I shouted from the back. "I have to turn on the air conditioning to make it stop," he said. "Well then, stop again and turn it on," I said, "but you're going to kill us with the smoke."

There were many interesting moments as we pursued our new path. When we arrived for one meeting in a city called Barquisimeto, there were only three people. Veronica wondered if we would skip the city and go on to the next. "No," I said, "we're going to do it with those three people." We did the meeting, and with the gifts we had brought along for the raffle, we handed one to each of the attendees. Those three people decided to join the business and, in time, became big leaders. It was a critical lesson. We reached a point where if only one person showed up, we would present our business plan to that one person because behind that one person could be a big leader. That's how the business was built — with one car, one trip, and one person at a time. By the time January rolled around, we each had a new car.

KNOWING YOUR WORTH

THE BEGINNING OF ANGELS

Before there were the mornings pushing that old, red Cavalier through the parking lot until the engine turned over, and before the road trips on a run-down bus, the plan for my first direct sales business started on a napkin.

When it became clear that I had no option but to leave SwissJust and go off on my own, I invited an old friend named David Calanche to coffee. David had supported and accompanied me in previous projects, especially during my moments of failure when I was turned away by others and left all alone. Now he worked in a company that I thought could be a starting point. I explained my situation and asked him to explain his company's business plan. Without hesitating for a moment, David took a napkin and began to write, plotting out what would become the start of my new company. That napkin is framed and hangs in my office to remind me where I come from and so I never forget those who helped me on my way to success. All the steps seemed easy enough. The difficult thing was finding a way to secure financial capital to form a company and manufacture its products to market them in Venezuela. I told Leudin I would talk to my brother.

My first goal had been to get my brother to believe in me. It isn't easy to put your capital in a failed person. I decided to talk to my brother Jesus Urdaneta, whose nickname was Chucho. "I have a business," I told him. "Do you want to invest with me?" The truth was, I didn't have a business at all. I had the idea in my mind and the guidance from David on a coffee shop napkin. I explained my plan to Chucho, including what was happening at David's company, and that since I had already been in the direct sales market, I had a lot of people who trusted me. Thankfully, my brother trusted me too. "Let's do business," he told me. He was eager to share the news. "C'mon," he said, "let's tell some of our brothers." When we told our younger brother, Leonardo, he was all in. "Let's get Edixon," he said. So in October 2001, we started Angels. Jesus, Edixon, Leonardo, and I each held a 25 percent stake in the business, but my brothers were involved in their own ventures, so they helped with the investment and I was in charge of the day-to-day operations and the decisions to get Angels off the ground.

Across the Caribbean Sea in Miami, Ray was studying for business school and working. After rough beginnings in the United States, when he slept under his cousin's staircase and worked at Sears with no car and no money, Ray had become something of an entrepreneur himself. For a while, he and Carolina traded in their jobs at Sears and McDonald's for positions at a telemarketing company, where they pushed credit cards for Capital One. Carolina worked on the Spanish side and

KNOWING YOUR WORTH

Ray took a job in the English department, which earned an extra dollar per hour. Eventually, that became tiring. "My brain is going to fry," he told Carolina. He bought an $800 Mitsubishi Eclipse, started buying perfumes and sunglasses at a wholesaler, and went door-to-door selling them. Instead of making $250 a week, he could make $250 with a few sales. When Ray left Venezuela for Miami, I was at my lowest moment. I had nothing to offer him financially, but I had instructed him to be on the lookout for opportunities. There was a growing business in Venezuela centered on collections, or kits, of products. Companies would put forty or so related products into a box and sell them for about $700. It worked like this: the direct sales company would get the the kits that came in a box from the manufacturer and sell them on credit to the sales force for $500 per box. The salespeople would make weekly or biweekly payments and keep the $200 profit. If the salesperson paid on time, they would be incentivized. When Ray went to Miami, I told him about the collections business model. He not only understood the model but had successfully used it himself to earn money to buy Carolina's plane tickets to Miami. "See if you can find something to sell," I told him.

Ray had been in Miami for a year when I called him after my meeting with the owner of SwissJust. "Listen, remember that idea?" I asked him. "Chucho told me he can invest. Why don't you come up with something to sell?" I thought we might do something like Victoria's Secret did with lingerie, which was popular in Venezuela at the time. As I went about convincing Veronica, Dubi, and Jose Luis to join the sales force, it turned out Ray wasn't fully convinced. When I called back the second time, I found out he hadn't made any progress. "Did you find some things?" I asked him. "I haven't had time," he told me. I waited a while longer before calling a third time. "Listen, if you can't find anything, Jesus has someone living in Los Angeles, and he has an idea for a clothing line," I said. "We're just going to go there." Ray was adamant he'd come up with an idea. "No, no, no," he said. "Give me a couple of weeks. I'll find something."

Over the days and weeks that followed, Ray would go to Walmart in Miami and look through products, reading the fine print on the back to see who manufactured them. The Internet wasn't very big then, so his research took time. He would read the manufacturing labels of all kinds of products that lined the shelves — clothes, shampoo, lotion, and perfume — to find out who manufactured and distributed them. As he began cold-calling distributors and explaining what he wanted to do, one of them offered some advice. "What you're looking for is a private label manufacturer," he told him. "Really? What's that?" Ray asked. "You go there and they make whatever you want,"

KNOWING YOUR WORTH

he said. Ray was familiar with reselling products. He had once borrowed his mother's credit card on a trip to Miami and brought Nike and Adidas shoes and clothing back to Venezuela to resell. He had recently done the same with perfume and sunglasses in Miami. Buying these boxes was popular in Venezuela, so it seemed like a good idea. Ray drove around Miami to different private label manufacturers and knocked on doors in pursuit of an opportunity. Then one day he finally called me with his plan. "This is the idea," I remember him telling me. "We can make our own brand." I wasn't convinced. "No, that's too hard," I told him. "How are we going to do that?" His answer was simple, "You go to a factory," he said. So Jesus and I traveled to Miami to meet with Ray and research his idea. Ray was convinced that we should use a US manufacturer because the quality of US-made products was well known in Venezuela, which would start our company in a positive light. Jesus and I stayed at a low-cost Days Inn, and the next day Ray took us around to three factories he had scouted out. The prices were amazing! We all liked B&R Products, which is the factory we ended up acquiring twelve years later. I remember high-fiving in the parking lot after we found B&R. There was real money in this business idea. The next day, before leaving Miami, Jesus said, "Let's go to the mall." I was in no financial position to go shopping. "No, you go ahead," I told him. "I don't have any money." He opened his wallet and handed me a hundred dollar bill. With it, I purchased a gift for my daughter back home.

That's how I started my first direct sales company. I didn't even have my own one hundred dollars But I was willing to sacrifice whatever it was going to take to make the dream happen. I started making my dream even though I had no money of my own and the odds were against my success. It would be difficult but not impossible.

What Ray, Jesus, and I settled on was an eighteen-product kit filled mostly with body lotions and body mists. I remember telling the manufacturer that assisted us, B&R Products, that we wanted to start by purchasing one shipping container of merchandise each month. When we told him about the plan, he started laughing at us, saying, "A lot of people come over here telling the same story." I told him, "But we are going to do it." In the years that followed, we peaked at purchasing fifty containers each month. With time, Angels began growing, and growing, and growing, and I slowly invited each of my brothers who invested to come work with me. It was a lot of work to run the business by myself. At first, everything was great, but with time, having four decision-makers became a problem. Family businesses experience cycles of both feast and famine. In almost all cases business growth is due to vision, leadership, dedication, and the dream of its founder, who, by developing the company from scratch, knows its operation, finances, clients, and market. It's important not to lose the dream and the vision required to reach the next level and the reinvestment necessary to generate innovative projects that allow the business to grow and remain competitive. It's very difficult for other people to understand your dreams and goals, and even more so if each person has different objectives.

MONEY AND POWER

There are things we must remain conscious of so we don't lose focus. We have to respect money and power. If you allow money to dominate you, you can lose your focus, you can compromise your principles, and you can hurt your values. If you allow power to dominate you, you can lose your modesty, and you may not achieve the best opportunities in front of you. When either money or power gets out of alignment in our lives, we put relationships at risk.

I learned this lesson during my downfall, and it was a mistake I didn't want to repeat. It can be easy to become complacent when success comes. There is a phrase that says, "The greatest enemy of tomorrow's success is today's success." Success in our lives should not be a destination, but a daily process. When we reach one goal and stop or get too comfortable, we risk waking up one day and wondering what happened. Success is not money, or power, or happiness. Success comes in many ways each day as we continue on our journey, following our passions toward our dreams.

To return to John C. Maxwell, in his renowned book *The Success Journey*, he defines success as three steps:

1. Knowing your purpose in life.
2. Growing to reach your maximum potential.
3. Sowing seeds that benefit others.

Maxwell goes on to write,
You can see by this definition why success is a journey rather than a destination. No matter how long you live or what you decide to do in life, you will never exhaust your capacity to grow toward your potential or run out of opportunities to help others. When you see success as a journey, you'll never have the problem of trying to "arrive" at an elusive final destination. And you'll never find yourself in a position where you have accomplished some final goal, only to discover that you're still unfulfilled and searching for something else to do.

KNOWING YOUR WORTH

When I left Tupperware, I lost my focus and fell into bad habits and learned that success was not being the #1 distributor or becoming a millionaire. In reality, what had fulfilled me all those years was the process of getting to the top of direct sales, not the fanciful final destination. It took hitting rock bottom to realize that my one True North was direct sales. It took failing to realize that I wasn't happy being successful when watching other people lose. I found out you cannot achieve success alone; success takes teamwork. When my brothers and I were unified as a team, everything flowed, and Angels was truly marvelous. Everything began to crumble when we started deviating from our one common path and going our own directions. The pivotal moment of my time at Angels came when I received a letter that my brothers were going to get financing from a bank to get capital to diversify the business. I had grand plans of extravagant promotions to grow the sales force and expand the business. It was clear we had different visions. It's important to know that when everyone isn't on the same path, sometimes it's best to stop and reevaluate where you are and where you want to go, then get back on the right path. It doesn't mean a particular person is right or wrong, but success comes when a team is in sync and moving toward the same goal. I learned in that moment that the key to success is always emphasizing the value of the people around you.

REBEL LEADERSHIP

Not everybody has the same definition of success, and that's OK! Our idea of success comes from where we're trying to go. It goes back to the question, What is your passion? Maybe there was a day when I thought success was simply building a big direct sales business and becoming a millionaire. But even if I thought that defined success, when I left Tupperware, I learned firsthand that, for me at least, success was more elusive than the money or power it granted me. People talk all the time about not making the same mistake twice. We must live and learn from our mistakes and failures. Looking back, I don't see it as I was right and my brothers were wrong. We just saw life differently; we had different ideas of where we wanted to go, and I found that success comes more easily when you're focused on one goal and one destination. For me, a successful direct sales business was no longer about making big money but about building a big company.

Most of the time as humans we want things to work. Maybe we force some things to work even though we know from the beginning it isn't the right way or isn't the right path. Stop for a minute and think: Are you aligned on your path toward success? Or are you stuck trying to force something to work? At the end of the day, what I knew could happen wound up happening. We established Angels in 2001, and in its first four years, it

KNOWING YOUR WORTH

operated like a dream. Working alongside my brothers and building something great in Venezuela holds an important place in my life and it's a big reason I've been able to achieve what I have since. But by 2005, I was beginning to create the next movie in my head. I hesitated leaving the company I built with my brothers, but when I saw the letter with an ultimatum, it became clear to me what I had to do. For the second time, I picked up the phone and called Ray in Miami to propose we start another business.

Ray and I created a plan, and from one day to another, I gathered my team and told them I was leaving. Then I made one of the most difficult calls to my brother Chucho.

"I'm leaving," I said. "I'm starting my own business."

CHAPTER 9

RETURNING TO SUCCESS

THERE WAS no turning back when I walked into the hotel conference room in Maracaibo on that day in 2005. The planning was done and the decision had been made. All that remained was the announcement. I gathered my close leaders and shut the door.

"I'm done here," I told them. "If you want to stay at Angels, that's fine, no problem. Whoever wants to come with me, I have my new business in the ballroom next door."

I turned and walked out, entering a nearby ballroom, which I had booked previously. I'd split from Angels to form a new company in the direct sales industry but with a brand-new name — Illusions. From the ballroom next door to Angels' meeting, I called my brother and broke the news to him. Eight months prior, I had started building a strategy, involving only a few employees to search for an office and to build a new operating system for the new company. Because the planning was secret, it caused a lot of stress, which meant it was a difficult period, but I knew it was the right decision. I felt as if the future of the company, the future of my employees, the future of my children, and my own future were at stake, and it was up to me to take care of everything. My brothers' initial reactions to Illusions were difficult. It was hard for them to understand, but later, each one started his own successful business, for which I thank God.

When I separated from Angels, nobody outside of my family and inner circle believed in me. Only my children and my sister Yixa and her husband, David. People told me I wasn't capable of running my own direct sales business because I didn't know about business management. The lesson in all of this is to take inspiration in what you believe in and what you want to obtain. Many people didn't believe in me or believe that I would succeed, and I faced a lot of criticism, but if I had not broken off from Angels, MONAT wouldn't exist today. It was about my True North and following what I believed I needed to achieve.

I've faced plenty of criticism and rejection during my journey. Rejection reveals itself in many forms in our lives. Sometimes it can be as obvious as getting turned down by the college you applied to or told you weren't

RETURNING TO SUCCESS

qualified for the job you chased. Sometimes it can be as subtle as someone questioning your dream or not believing in you or your vision. I previously told the story of when my uncle told me that although my brothers had finished their studies at the university, I was a good-for-nothing loser. That was a moment that inspired me, and I have never forgotten it. I remember telling myself that I would show my uncle that he was completely mistaken. When people criticized and mocked me and told me I was a crazy dreamer because I was thinking of accomplishing big things, those memories challenged and motivated me. When you live with rejection, you realize that it's important to trust in yourself, to believe in what you think, and to not allow anything or anybody to make you lose your focus. That happened when I started with Tupperware, it happened when I returned to direct sales, and it happened when I started on the path of opening my own business. I remember a friend telling me that opening a direct sales company was too difficult, and on many occasions, they suggested I shouldn't do it. I made the decision to do it anyway because I was convinced that I could.

When I started in my early business projects, I failed in many of them until I realized that there was something that was holding me back: I wasn't in love with them. All I was chasing was money. When I began in direct sales with Tupperware, it was about money, but the difference was that I fell in love with what I was doing and I developed a passion for direct sales. I believe that is crucial. Passion has always been decisive to be able to overcome later adversities. This is worth repeating: you have to be in love with what you're doing. You have to feel passionate and have a bigger purpose. That's the secret to overcoming rejection. When you're not passionate about something, it's no surprise that at the first sign of rejection, you quit, because it didn't have a bigger purpose for you. It's natural for the fear of failure to creep into your mind when others criticize your decisions or reject you. Success and failure go hand in hand. You have to fall in love with your dream. Once you do, rejection and doubt from other people become secondary. There are so many things that have happened to me for the best. There has always been a positive reason and a positive why.

I didn't know what to expect when Ray and I split off the company, but I saw the doubters as a new challenge. I invited Veronica, Dubi and Jose Luis, Marjorie, and Kathy, who is my right hand when it comes to analytics, data, and strategy, to join me as leaders at Illusions, and thankfully they all agreed and are my partners to this day.

The time came and our new company was born when I had to start again, but now with more passion and enthusiasm developing the appropriate behaviors, creating a team that believed in my dreams, looking for leaders throughout the country, traveling nonstop, developing administrative staff, and learning to delegate. I always understood that to achieve my goal I had to form a team with my values — loyal, upright, and tireless. It was time to continue with the original goal: to develop not just a company but a corporation in the field of direct selling.

NO SUCCESS WITHOUT SACRIFICE

Our success building a direct sales company didn't come easy, not for me or anyone who stayed with me through every step along the way. There were moments when I hit rock bottom and others where I was on my way back to the top of direct sales. But the truth is, moments of success came through days, weeks, months, and years of sacrifice and enduring many failures and much rejection. Success is not an instant journey. No one just hits the jackpot. (Believe me, I learned that the hard way!) Success takes time, patience, and a lot of sacrifice. It is moving toward your goals and dreams one day after the next. And it rarely, if ever, comes in a straight line.

It might feel like leaving Angels one day and starting another direct sales company the next was easy, but it was a struggle. From my start in direct sales in 1982 to building my first company at Angels and everything that came after, I have faced many challenges, taken many risks, and made many sacrifices. When we started on our own in 2001, there was a time when we completely put aside things such as vacations because we didn't have time for fun. We knew we had to fight hard to succeed. Whether it was 1982, 2001, 2005, or 2014, when we started on our own again, results came only after constant sacrifice, suffering, and distress. That's the way that success was — and still is — earned. The effort, the suffering, and the stress were always present, and our new company had to defeat all those situations to get where we wanted to go.

On social media today, everybody posts their great, beautiful, successful moments: the nice vacation, the new car, the great achievement. With a little help from my children, I've gotten on social media and seen many positives, notably the ability to connect with our sales force around the world. But I've also seen the paradigm it has created when it comes to success. Many people fall into a trap today thinking social media is a real, true representation of life, but when was the last time you saw photos of failure, sacrifice, distress? When we started Illusions, we worked full time seven days a week, traveled long hours on the Venezuelan highways every day, and stayed in any cheap hotel we could find between cities. It took time to get where we wanted to go. Today

RETURNING TO SUCCESS

many people see something and want it for themselves, but they don't want to endure what it takes to get it. They see only the result of the unglamorous moments nobody shows. If I had Instagram when I became the #1 Tupperware distributor in the 1980s, I might have posted about the car I earned or my trip to Puerto Rico, but would I have posted about walking from house to house knocking on doors or sitting on the bus with my two pink bags? Today there are many glamorous moments, but they weren't always abundant. And success can be fleeting. Even today, the road ahead requires moments of great sacrifice.

    We had to work with a lot of limitations at the beginning. I remember when Veronica would take the bus at night to be able to make all of the trips and meetings during the day. To be able to develop the business, we traveled a lot in the beginning, spending hours in the car or on a bus traveling from Maracaibo to cities both big and small across the country. One day we had our first event at noon in a city four hours from Maracaibo, followed by a stop in another town on the way back. When the first event was done, we would eat and then get back in the car to rush toward the second stop of the day. It was stressful, and in the middle of our drive to the second city I felt a stomach ache. Initially, I thought I could handle it. "We need to make it to the event," I said. But I just couldn't do it. We pulled off and stopped at a gas station so I could run into the restroom. I was wearing a suit and tie, and my shirt was long. In a moment of desperation, I sat down on the toilet without realizing the white shirt was still under me — it was like a filter. When I stood up, I realized my shirt was a disaster. I was so desperate to make it to the next stop that I removed the tie, took off the shirt and started washing it in the sink. It wouldn't go away. The shirt was yellow and it smelled awful. I put the shirt and tie back on and went back to the car. "My love," I told Leudin, "it's a disaster." I asked for some perfume to cover up the smell. "We can't go there like this," she told me. I was adamant. "We will make it," I said, "and we will do it." When we arrived, there were four hundred people waiting for us. I wasn't going to leave these people waiting. "Nobody gets close to me on the stage," I warned my leaders. I wanted to focus on my speech. The presentation was successful and we headed home.

As the new business grew, rewarding the salespeople for selling our boxes was critical. I tasked Ray with finding rewards we could purchase in Miami. One time, he found a number of coffee makers we could purchase as prizes for salespeople. When the boxes arrived in Venezuela, we knew they were refurbished as they were a great deal, but we had a surprise when we opened them because many of them were still dirty.

RETURNING TO SUCCESS

"The coffee makers have coffee in them," I told Ray. We had no choice. The corporate employees got together and cleaned them so we could give them away. Another time, Ray was able to purchase used sound equipment, which not only sounded nice but was a popular item in Venezuela. The only problem was that half of the stereos sounded good and the other half sounded bad. We had to work with a sound technician to fix all of the equipment. All those problems were things the company went through as it was growing. The point is, don't allow obstacles to thwart your goals.

The first years of the new business were long and hard because money was tight. But everyone in the field and in the office worked as a team, a team that together was able to overcome adversity. I've always said that in order to develop leadership you have to have honesty, humbleness, fairness, and rectitude in everything you do. That was one of the biggest lessons I learned from my years of experience starting and building a direct sales business. When people believe in you, they follow you. When people admire you, they follow you. When you respect people and you get them to respect you, they will follow you. When you are inspired by someone that is guiding you, for me that has all the power in the world. That is what helped me make the transition in the short term to achieve spectacular results. I was able to overcome so much in my forty years in direct sales only because I knew those moments of sacrifice or failure would be a part of my path. You need to struggle, be persistent, and be consistent to achieve results. You also need passion and love for what you're doing. Believe that you can change your quality of life and also that of the people around you.

THE BEGINNING OF L'EUDINE

When we started our new direct sales company, I had to redirect my goals and objectives with humility and great wisdom since all the decisions were mine to make. The successes and failures of the company depended on me. I had to develop the skills of a fearless leader since behind me there was a large number of leaders who counted on me and our company to survive. I went back to my roots, to when I had wanted to be an entrepreneur and have my own direct sales company.

Something that has always helped me and that I pass on to all my staff in different countries is that to achieve a goal in life, you have to believe it, then the rest will come — hard work, discipline, perseverance, and a good product. If you believe it, you will achieve it, I guarantee it. I believed I could be an entrepreneur and that I could have my own direct sales company.

RETURNING TO SUCCESS

I want to reaffirm what I always say in my talks and at conferences: if you behave like a leader and act every day with faith, you will achieve success.

We as a company had to make strong decisions, create new strategies, reinvest in new product ideas, and redirect objectives, and that doesn't stop. There are always new challenges, whether you're at the beginning of your journey to success or ten years down the road. There will always be new challenges to confront. But in each situation there is a solution. And if we don't have it, we look for it. And if it doesn't exist, we invent it. But let's go forward! We are not going to allow anybody to steal our dream.

As we pushed forward in 2005, we created a unique plan with fabulous compensation margins and transformed the system with gifts for achievements and punctuality in payment that revolutionized the market. We worked hard to consolidate successful leaders in each of the twenty-three states across Venezuela, working on the premise of win-win. For us to win, our people had to win too. If in any promotion or launch that rule was not fulfilled, we didn't go forward with it.

Never think that while you're making money, the rest of the people don't matter. If you focus only on yourself, you will then be creating a business for the short term, but when you create a team for the long term, everyone wins. If you believe in something and work hard to consolidate those principles in your leaders, much of the way is won. What began as a dream became a great reality, achieving a sales force of more than one hundred thousand throughout Venezuela, helping them achieve and build their own dreams and strengthen their status in life. When you dream big and work hard, the path opens. We grew a lot in our home country and decided to venture into new markets. We knew we had a difficult task and had no experience expanding into new markets, but we weren't afraid of the challenge. Life belongs to the daring, to those who dare to seek what belongs to them. Life belongs to the brave.

By 2007, we were already thinking about expanding outside of Venezuela into other Latin America markets. From the time I began my career in Tupperware, I always dreamed of going to Mexico, where direct sales were huge. When we started our adventure into these new markets, we were halted by one of those challenges: the brand name Illusions was already taken. But as I said before, every situation has a solution. And this challenge in particular ended up being a huge blessing. We decided to come up with a brand that nobody would have. We hired an agency to come and do a brand refresh for us. After spending time with us, asking about our values, our story, and learning our family dynamics, they created a

RETURNING TO SUCCESS

presentation for us where they did incredible visual work, but they also surprised us all when they used Leudin's name to come up with our new name. We thought it was amazing, elegant, and beautiful.

That's how we came up with L'eudine, adding an *e* to the name of the person who was alongside me every step of the way on my journey back to direct sales. That's how we rebranded again. L'eudine Global was born, and it still carries on as part of the family business today.

In 2009 we went international, starting with Colombia, then moving into Mexico, and finally expanding into Ecuador. We had high expectations and invested the most money in Mexico. We all traveled to Mexico together for the opening, but from day one we were losing money. The currency began to crumble, and because we didn't know the market, we made a lot of mistakes. We tried to make it work for many years, losing $3.5 million before it became too much and forced us to shut down operations in the country. It wasn't until several years later that I saw this as a blessing. If we had found success in a big direct sales market like Mexico, we probably would have never set our eyes on the United States.

Many times in life we face obstacles, or worse, failures, and can't seem to find an immediate "why." It isn't easy, but these challenges can become blessings. I want to share with you actions that you most likely know and practice in your life, but they helped me find my way on my various journeys:

- Believe it.
- Prioritize.
- Set goals.
- Never get discouraged.
- Be persistent.
- Finish what you start.
- Don't let anyone steal your dreams.

The person who perseveres wins, and that is what happened to us. L'eudine became a great phenomenon in the field of direct sales in Venezuela, ranking among the top organizations in the country and growing to become a $200 million organization operating across Latin America. The reality is, both failures and successes serve as experience. I'm not afraid of failing. I'm more afraid of not trying and wondering what could have been and was not. Life is made of attempts and failures, and only adventurers go where no one else has gone.

CHAPTER 10

MY COUNTRY IN RUINS

I SAT in my bulletproof car outside of the restaurant in Maracaibo as one of my bodyguards went ahead to sweep the building. The message from the Venezuelan criminals was clear: they were going to kidnap me. Either I had to pay or they would kill me. When I first heard about the threat, I didn't pay much attention to it, but as the rumors grew louder, I was forced to accept the reality that I was in danger. Sitting in the middle of three armored vehicles, I waited for the all clear so that I could get in. My lead escort parked in front and two others trailed behind. I sat in the middle of the three armored vehicles and waited. Despite having achieved my dream in Venezuela by building a direct sales corporation in my homeland and across the Americas, the moment forced me to face a grim realization. Amid my

REBEL LEADERSHIP

success, I had become a prisoner in my own country.

The signs of economic and political unrest in Venezuela were already evident by that time in 2007. The early years of the Hugo Chávez presidency were met by rampant oil production that had long made Venezuela a thriving economy and one of the richest countries in Latin America. In the early 2000s, Chávez enacted what became known as Bolivarian missions that were aimed at improving economic and social conditions for the country's poor and working classes, from free health clinics to subsidized food to educational programs and low-income housing. In the years that followed, poverty rates plummeted by more than 20 percent and Venezuela thrived in many ways. At the same time, first Angels and then L'eudine took off. By 2006, L'eudine built a sales force of more than one hundred thousand people and became one of the biggest direct sales corporations across Venezuela.

Then everything began to crumble. As a petrostate with 99 percent of its export revenue coming from oil and with growing debt, the warning signs of a collapse were evident even before the fall. When the 2008 global financial crisis hit, Venezuela's dependence on oil and a significant turn toward authoritarianism by the Chávez regime sent the economy spiraling out of control. Oil prices crashed and the billions of dollars Chávez had directed toward social programs began to dry up. In

MY COUNTRY IN RUINS

2008, inflation in Venezuela crossed 30 percent, crippling the economy. Millions of Venezuelans who had relied on the oil industry for their livelihoods or who had reaped the benefits from the welfare programs funded by a glut of money from the oil industry began to sink into poverty and the crime rate spiked. Chávez, meanwhile, began his push toward authoritarian power. He took control of the Supreme Court, began the process of nationalizing hundreds of businesses, enacted censorship, and introduced a constitutional amendment to abolish presidential term limits.

The situation in Maracaibo had gotten out of control, not only because the economy was crumbling and the political landscape was tenuous but also because L'eudine was at the height of its success and hugely popular. Everyone knew that the shipments of products arriving from Miami to the port of Maracaibo were destined for L'eudine. Luis Urdaneta had become a household name.

By the end of 2008 and beginning of 2009, Venezuela's relationship with the United States had worsened, and foreign currencies — including the US dollar — were taken out of circulation in the country. Since all of L'eudine's products were imported, it meant our operations were almost paralyzed. In the middle of a global financial crisis, with Venezuela's inflation skyrocketing and the bolívares exchange rate to the US dollar doubling, the company already faced an uphill climb, and now we couldn't access money. The economy was spiraling downward and the odds were being stacked against us. But I decided to make a big change and redefine the business to keep it operational despite the setbacks.

During the political turmoil in Venezuela and when great devaluation came, prompting the US dollar's disappearance from banks, I was forced to turn to the black market. I would collect bolívares from our sales and take them to the black market to exchange them for US dollars. There wasn't any other way to do it because banks couldn't do it. The move was risky because to make the exchange you first had to hand over the bolívares to swap them for US dollars. We exchanged millions of dollars monthly through the black market. It was very stressful and intense, but we had no choice if we wanted to keep the company running. One day, I gave a man enough bolívares to be exchanged for $1 million. He took the bolívares and disappeared. I never saw him again. I lost $1 million. That was the first time I thought about leaving Venezuela.

It wasn't long after that the threats began. The criminals knew I was a millionaire and therefore a target. In Venezuela, violent crime is common, and often wealthy businessmen or their family members are kidnapped

MY COUNTRY IN RUINS

and held hostage in exchange for ransom or are even threatened with assassination. It became clear to me that my country was in ruins, and I couldn't live like that. I decided that one way or another I would find a solution. So I sat outside the restaurant waiting to meet a man who could help.

FACING DANGER IN MY HOMELAND

When my bodyguards intercepted an extortion attempt, I could no longer ignore the threats. I couldn't risk something happening to me — or worse, my family. I was already spending thousands of dollars on security details to protect me and my family, and they had become aware of the kidnapping plot against me. Now I had no other choice. I needed a godfather.

Through my bodyguards I was able to contact a person who knew the people who wanted to kidnap me. Maybe you've seen *The Godfather*, the movie where a character named Vito Corleone builds a mafia empire. Vito is the godfather, the boss of all bosses. I needed a similar person who could help, like a mafia boss or godfather in Maracaibo. When I got in touch with the man, the first thing he said was, "I'll protect you and I'll help you to negotiate." But it came with a cost. "We have to go to a couple of well-known restaurants in the city. People have to see you with me." I didn't want to spend time with him, but his strategy was to let the would-be kidnappers see me with him so they knew he was protecting me. He was a very powerful person in the crime world, so our presence together would intimidate those who threatened me and cause them to back down. For some time, I went from restaurant to restaurant across Maracaibo with him to give off the impression I hung out with worse criminals than those who threatened me. After spending some time with the godfather, he contacted the group that wanted to kidnap or kill me and negotiated for them to stop. I don't know how much he paid them, but I paid him $3 million over the next four years to protect my family and me and help us avoid more extortion. It was what I had to do to keep my family safe in Venezuela.

Those moments were almost like living in a movie. Leudin and I had seven bodyguards and our daughter Lu, who lived in her own place, had four bodyguards of her own. It was hard to know if a person was honest or not. One of the most traumatic moments came when Lu was eighteen years old. Her bodyguards drove her to gymnastics and a group of men started threatening one of them. While Lu was inside, her bodyguard was shot and killed. It was a dark moment of my life in Venezuela. Lu's bodyguard was someone I appreciated, and he, like all the others who protected my family and others across

MY COUNTRY IN RUINS

Venezuela, Latin America, and even the United States, gave his life to keep us safe.

What finally began to push me to leave Venezuela was when it wasn't just the common criminals coming after me and the company, but also the white-collar criminals. Government officials arrived at my office and demanded that I either pay them some large amount of money or I would be audited. Since the company had so many imports coming into the Maracaibo port, the military had the maximum authority. When people from the military came to the office, they demanded a commission for each shipping container that arrived in Venezuela. The government, the military, and the mayor of Maracaibo were bandits who came to the company in search of money. Every situation caused more frustration. Little by little I began to reach the breaking point of saying, "No more! I'm not taking this!"

When the top militaries of the government started calling me, I sent Kathy, one of my best and most trusted employees in Venezuela, to Caracas to negotiate. Kathy not only negotiated the commission for our imports but also became a good friend of the general. One Friday night I met the general in Caracas for dinner and drinks when he noticed my white Porsche Cayenne. There were no Porsches in Venezuela, so I had equipped one in Miami with a spectacular sound system and every other available option and then imported it into Venezuela. "Wow," the general said to me, "what a beauty." I didn't hesitate. "You know what, it's yours," I told him. "It's a present." At that moment, the car meant nothing to me because I needed the general more than I needed the Porsche. I thought, "If I win this guy, the corrupt politicians will leave me alone." From then on, whenever I arrived in Caracas, the general would send me an escort of motorbikes and cars to take me to the airport. I felt like a big politician with vehicles escorting me everywhere I went in Maracaibo and Caracas.

I've said that there is a solution to every situation, but no matter what I did to keep my family safe or protect L'eudine from corruption and blocked imports, I couldn't control Venezuela's soaring inflation. In 2009, the country hit a recession. To keep L'eudine operating, I had to adjust the price of the product almost weekly, but inflation rose higher than the adjustments and it no longer made any sense. The business stopped being a business. I remember calling Ray in Miami and venting. The economy was getting worse and worse; it was becoming hard to find US dollars, even on the black market. The constant stress of extortion and intimidation to give away our earnings to people who didn't deserve it pushed me to a breaking point. Maybe the trouble made sense when there was a business, but when L'eudine stopped being profitable, there was no sense in facing the distress we were living. "I have to come to Miami," I told Ray in late 2009. "I have no other option."

COMING TO AMERICA

It's still hard to revisit this stage of my life. Having to leave my country, not because I wanted to but due to political reasons, generalized violence, and the silent loss of social and economic rights, was very hard. Giving up your roots, your customs, and above all, your family, is something I wouldn't want any human being to experience.

By this time, we already had an office in Miami. I love my country, but when your safety and that of your wife and youngest daughters, Luisana and Lu, is at stake, things change. Living surrounded by armed bodyguards, needing seven escorts to leave your office or go to dinner, and not being able to enjoy your freedoms is unimaginable. It's difficult to assume that reality, especially after building a business from zero and watching it grow. To accept that you have to let go and leave because there's no path ahead is hard to digest. Leaving my people and my company was extremely difficult. I learned the importance of always having your feet on the ground and accepting the situations that sometimes we don't want to see. I have made a lot of difficult decisions.

One of those was accepting the challenge of starting my career in direct sales. Another came in 1995 when I left Tupperware. When I was ruined and had to start again from zero, building a business from scratch wasn't easy. I risked starting a company and not knowing if it was going to succeed. But my eagerness and my desire to achieve great opportunities pushed me forward. In those situations, the one commonality was that I dared. I had the courage to make those decisions. When fear dominates you, you're always going to walk down the wrong path. That's why I always tell people to dare to make decisions regardless of if they are right or wrong. I truly believe that on many occasions that is what many people are lacking — to have the courage to dare.

I remember how difficult it was for me to make the decision to leave Venezuela behind, but I spoke to Ray and told him that the way I saw corrupt politicians running the country, there was no more opportunity for L'eudine. I decided I was going to go to the United States to search for an opportunity for a business that would give us the future we dreamed of. I've always been a big dreamer. Toward the end of my time in Maracaibo, I told Marjorie, one of my finance leaders at L'eudine, that I dreamed of going to Miami and starting a new direct sales business. "I dream of having a yacht, looking at my computer and organizing all the businesses while holding a cigar in my

MY COUNTRY IN RUINS

hand," I told her. I accepted the reality of the situation and I made the decision. I told my leaders in Venezuela that I was going to go through difficult times to search for the right path forward. Without knowing what I was going to do in Miami, I began thinking and dreaming about the business that was going to open the doors to the American Dream. That's why in my speeches I always say, "To achieve your dreams you have to believe in your dreams, focus, and have the courage to make difficult decisions." To be able to make the difficult decisions, you have to be ready. If I would have let fear control me, I might still be in Venezuela.

    I faced a lot of problems as I prepared to leave. I was leaving my business. I was leaving my home. I was leaving behind my extended family, including my brothers. On top of all that, Leudin didn't want to come. I still have many difficult memories from my decision to leave Venezuela. Leaving a life of success behind to come to America was difficult. But I went back to the same thing — having the courage to make difficult decisions. Making those decisions at the right time was an important part of my experience. We lived in a rented house in Venezuela, and Leudin and I argued almost every day because she didn't want to rent. It upset her all the time. "We deserve a house," she would tell me. "A home!" I told her many times, "I'm going to buy your beautiful house, but in

REBEL LEADERSHIP

Miami." When Ray moved to Miami and I visited him, I would say, "Let's drive around and see the most beautiful houses, because one of those houses will be mine."

I had finally purchased our home in Miami, but Leudin was still frustrated. I tried to sell her the idea that moving to Miami was something spectacular, but she didn't buy it. She didn't speak English and her entire family was in Venezuela. Complicating matters, getting a visa in Venezuela was expensive and complex if a person didn't own property in the United States. I still remember Leudin crying as we prepared to leave. It was like I was forcing her to go to a place where she didn't know anyone.

I struggled to let go of the company I had built in my homeland. For many months we talked about leaving for the United States, but I didn't want to give up control of L'eudine. Then came a family ski trip to Aspen, Colorado. Maybe it was God who nudged me over my skis and sent me tumbling down that snow hill, fracturing both ankles on the way down. The accident sent me to the hospital and forced me to stay in the United States for several months while I recovered. Back in Venezuela, the company kept running with Kathy, Marjorie, Dubi, Jose Luis, and Veronica. I realized for the first time that I didn't necessarily need to be in Venezuela for L'eudine to operate. "Okay," I thought, "I can go to the United States."

MY COUNTRY IN RUINS

That's when I bought the house in Miami.

I made a plan to convert as much stock as I could into cash to be able to make the trip to America and left two of the greatest leaders that I had in Venezuela to run the day-to-day operations. That day, Leudin, Luisana, my mother-in-law, and I left Maracaibo behind. Leudin cried as our bodyguards led us from the only home we had ever known together to the airport in Caracas. I looked down from thirty thousand feet above as we departed Caracas, flew out of Venezuela, and across the Caribbean Sea toward Miami. I was anxious about leaving Venezuela because of what I had lived, because of all the difficult situations I had to face. But I didn't regret anything. What I'm clear about is that God has reserved for you and me things that we can't even imagine. I always believe that the best is yet to come, that hope is ahead, and that the past is left behind. I knew there was a great opportunity ahead. So instead of suffering and regretting things I couldn't control in my business or in my life in Venezuela, I started turning the page quickly and focusing on what I wanted to achieve in America. It was time to undertake my dream in another country, and I had to do it with enthusiasm, courage, and above all, gratitude. I thank God, the United States, and its people for sheltering me and receiving me as one of them, and I will never know how to express my gratitude for what I received.

REBEL LEADERSHIP

When we reached Miami, I drove to the gas station and put gas in my car by myself. In Venezuela, I couldn't do that myself; my bodyguards had to do it because if I went to the gas station, I was taking a risk. During my final years in Venezuela, I lived in a prison. I'll never forget standing at the gas pump. I was free. After leaving my country, I had to start a new life. I needed to start thinking differently about managing the corporation and manufacturing from the new corporate office in Miami. Life puts people to the test every day, and I am no exception. We began to seek and develop what we had in our hands. We began to look forward in pursuit of the American Dream.

CHAPTER 11

FOR MY PEOPLE

SITTING AROUND the conference table in Miami, I stared down at the sheet of paper that lay in front of me. For many months we had done all we could to maintain the business in Venezuela. Every month the company was losing money, and now the finances said it could no longer continue. We owed $20 million. I knew this reality but in my heart didn't want to accept it. After a hard team meeting, we were left with no choice. "We have to close Venezuela," I told my corporate team.

When Leudin and I left Venezuela in 2009, the business had fallen roughly 70 percent compared to L'eudine's peak. As inflation continued to rise and the country sank into a recession, selling became more difficult. Unemployment in the country ran rampant, and we were losing members of the sales force left and right. When I arrived in Miami, I had thought about closing the company but never seriously considered it those first few months. There were too many people who depended on their income from L'eudine to support their lives and families. Our employees trusted that we were going to continue supporting them. So we kept the company going, even though we knew it was going to be an uphill battle because of everything happening. But as time wore on and the debt added up, there was no choice.

Operations had decreased significantly, but closing down in Venezuela still meant that between thirty thousand and forty thousand members of the sales force and another five hundred or so corporate employees of L'eudine would lose their livelihoods and be without a salary. We painfully discussed as a corporate team how we would announce our decision to leave the country. Members of my leadership team suggested that since I already lived in the United States, and because traveling to Venezuela could be dangerous, that we should release a letter or hold a video conference. "I cannot do this through a letter or a video call," I said. "I need to face my people. I owe them that." We talked about it many times, but there was no real decision to make. After everything these people had done for me, for the company, I needed to show my face.

When we arrived at the event we had prepared in Maracaibo, people from the sales force greeted me with similar messages. "Mr. Luis, we are counting on you," they said. "Everything will be better. Go ahead and make the changes you need to make. We're going to sell whatever you give us to sell as long as you don't close the business. That is our main source of income." One phrase in particular struck me. "If you ask us to sell those rocks," one person told me, "we will sell rocks." I gathered my leaders and corporate team behind the scenes. "I cannot do this. I cannot leave those people without any income," I said. "I wouldn't be here and I wouldn't have what I have today without those people. I will not leave them alone. Let's keep trying." The team, myself, and everybody understood there was no real path forward. Even the finances said it was impossible. But I didn't have the heart to shutter the business and to leave all those people behind. I don't know if I didn't have the courage to make the decision to leave or if I *had* the courage to continue losing money in order to stay. Whatever the case, we boarded the plane and flew back to Miami. I knew it was only a matter of time before everything would fall and the business would end, but for that moment at least we maintained the company to create income for those people.

    I never thought of doing anything other than direct sales. When I left the industry in the 1990s and subsequently hit rock bottom and was ruined, I realized I shouldn't have looked anywhere else. So when I arrived in the United States in 2009, my focus was on supporting and monitoring the business in Venezuela. By then we had expanded to Colombia, Ecuador, and Mexico, and I was searching to find ways to boost those markets. When we returned to Miami with the Venezuela market still open, I called Ray into my office and asked him to analyze our situation and look for alternatives that would help the corporation's finances. It was difficult to have patience during all those years as we searched, without luck, to find the optimal business plan. Our headache was worsened by the fact that every month during the next two years we suffered considerable losses. We discovered a harsh reality: the Latin American emerging markets were politically unstable markets with weak currencies. For the next couple of years, the company tumbled downward, losing another $8 million. Leaving L'eudine open was terribly expensive, but the value of gratitude was greater than money.

A NIGHTMARE BEFORE THE DREAM

I learned an important lesson when we landed in Miami: before achieving your American Dream you have to go through a nightmare. To say the least, starting fresh in the United States wasn't going to be easy. As the L'eudine leadership team began to debate the next steps for the company and as Ray and I researched the possibility of starting a new business venture entirely in America,

FOR MY PEOPLE

across Miami our manufacturing partner B&R struggled to keep the factory running.

From the day I empowered Ray to find a manufacturing partner in the United States so my brothers and I could start Angels, B&R had become a critical component of our success. When we came up with the idea of creating private label beauty and wellness products, the team at B&R took the idea and made it a reality. From 2002 until 2012, B&R was very loyal. The owner of the company had stood by our side when we left Angels to start L'eudine, and the partnership thrived. B&R met our needs when we ramped up from one shipping container of products each month to many containers at our peak. And when we began to reinvest profits to create new, innovative products, they provided the expertise and know-how to help us make it happen. But by 2012, as the Venezuelan currency continued to spiral into a progressive and uncontrollable devaluation, L'eudine and B&R were practically paralyzed. Millions of dollars' worth of products were sitting in inventory, bills were owed to various suppliers in China and the United States, and the factory, which relied almost exclusively on L'eudine, was practically shut down.

When the business in Venezuela fell near the end of 2012, our orders from B&R plummeted toward zero. It wasn't long after that the owner called Ray looking for financial assistance. "I bought some materials," he said. "Can you give me an advance?" The factory had fallen into debt and the owner had overspent. We agreed to provide the next month's payment in advance. Not long after, he called Ray again asking for another advance. We agreed to wire another payment. When he called a third time, we hesitated. We had already loaned the owner $3.5 million. "Ray, we can't continue lending money," I said. "He doesn't have clients and the cost is too high to maintain." Even if we supported what we thought we needed to in order to maintain the factory for our hopeful American Dream, B&R didn't have money to pay us back.

"I'm going over there," Ray said. We couldn't understand why there was so much need for inventory. L'eudine had lost more than seventy thousand members of the sales force from its peak and sales had slowed considerably. Ray left the office and drove across Miami to the factory. "How much do you have in inventory?" he asked the owner. "Let me see." They had nearly $2 million worth of L'eudine products sitting in the warehouse. "Where's the money we've been giving you?" Ray asked. It turned out that B&R was deep in debt. It was a disaster. When Ray returned to the office he told me about the situation. We invited the owner to our office in Doral, Florida. "I think we've supported you enough and I truly do not see a future for your factory," I told him. "You don't have

FOR MY PEOPLE

production, your monthly expenses are very high and you don't have a project for the future to be able to have success in your factory."

When I moved to Miami in search of a new business, it was never a dream or a goal to own a manufacturing plant. More than being part of an American Dream, helping B&R was simply a circumstance that came up that we had to work with to be able to achieve the business that we wanted to achieve in the United States. At that time in 2012, neither Ray nor I were thinking about keeping the B&R factory. We just wanted to help the owner overcome the situation. "Look, I'm going to propose the following," I told the owner as we sat in the office. "I'm going to send my people to do an audit on the current situation of the company, and once this is assessed, we can sit down again. But I cannot continue injecting money and lending money under a situation that is precarious." At first, he didn't want to allow the audit. He declined our offer and left upset. "If he doesn't accept this," I told Ray, "we're not going to lend him any more money." Two weeks later, he returned to negotiate with us. We had just the one request. "We want to audit your business," we told him again. Finally, he relented.

When we received the results from the B&R audit, we were shocked. It was worse than we had expected. Not only did the owner owe us the $3.5 million we had loaned him, but he owed on credit cards and had debts of millions with his suppliers. We scheduled a meeting with the owner. I was upset with him. "You lied to us," I told him. "You didn't tell us you owed your suppliers millions of dollars." We had no idea how we were ever going to recover our money. When the meeting finished, I said to Ray, "We have no other option. We need to ask him to sell us the factory." The only path I could see to recover our money was to buy the factory and machinery, negotiate with the suppliers, and see how, little by little, we could go about reviving the business. "That's risky," Ray said. "It's almost crazy." There was no other choice.

    We negotiated and eventually settled on purchasing 80 percent of B&R and leaving the owner a 20 percent stake in the company. In reality, that was nothing. There was *no* money. All B&R had at that moment was debt. When we went to the bank to hammer out the deal, L'eudine's accountant was concerned with the amount of B&R's debt. In order to lower the debt-to-capital ratio, we had to leave the owner with just a sliver of the company — he would get only 1 percent. It wasn't ideal, but it needed to happen because the bank wouldn't take on the risk. We talked to the owner and explained the situation. We promised that while the agreement would guarantee him only 1 percent, we would eventually make it work so he got the 20 percent we initially promised. "Sign this, but

FOR MY PEOPLE

20 percent is yours," we said. "You need to trust us." He trusted us, signed the document, and kept 1 percent of B&R. We took control and continued to operate both L'eudine and B&R.

When we assumed control of B&R, it was *not* the American Dream. It was a challenge that we stumbled upon. At that time, it was the American Nightmare. B&R had one small client. I remember the first month B&R's expenses totaled $300,000 and we earned roughly $50,000 from the client. We were losing money from the start. Ray warned that things were only going to get worse. "There is nothing to do, Son," I told him. "We have to continue forward." Now that we had a factory, it was clear that the manufacturing plant was going to become part of our future direct sales company in US, our Project USA dream. We continued investing and injecting money. We began speaking to B&R's suppliers, who were of course upset because they were owed millions. It was very clear that we had to negotiate with the suppliers because if there was no payment plan, the factory was going to have to close. Ray was able to negotiate a significant reduction in debts with the suppliers to allow B&R to continue. We endured a rough seven months before B&R became a godsend (which I'll tell you about next).

The original owner of B&R continued to work for us in the years that followed. Around 2019, Ray and I extended him an offer. "Look, let's do something," we said. "If you want to retire to your farm, we can purchase that 1 percent from you. We will purchase your 1% for the equivalent of the 20% of the value of the factory." Our new chief financial officer was flabbergasted. "Why are you doing that? You're crazy," he said. "Legally, you don't need to give it to him." He was right. According to the agreement, he owned only 1 percent. But our word was our word and B&R was a big reason we reached great success. "No," we said. "Let's give him what we offered, which is the equivalent of the 20%. Let's be fair." What I learned in that moment was the importance of strong leadership. If I want people to follow me, I need to show them how to be a leader with integrity and transparency. When you do the right thing, even when you face difficult moments, people will appreciate that integrity. Never take advantage of any situation. Values are important when things are difficult.

Not long after taking control of the B&R factory, I realized there was nothing else I could do to keep L'eudine operational. We owed millions and millions of dollars to different providers, and the business in Venezuela was on the brink of bankruptcy after four years of drought. We had a business with declining sales, a bankrupt factory, and a dark future ahead. In the end there was no other option. We were losing too much money; our debts were getting higher and higher. We had to leave the business in Venezuela behind. In 2012 I decided to close Venezuela. This time there was no going back. I may not have been able to see the positive in that moment, but as one door was closing at L'eudine, another was opening with B&R. At that moment in time, it felt like I was in the middle of a nightmare. But with time and perspective, I realized that those two conflicting moments were an opportunity. If B&R had never happened and L'eudine hadn't reach its end, we might still be in Venezuela. In the midst of despair, we were forced to seek opportunity. That crack in the proverbial B&R door was our gateway to the American Dream — we just had to chase it.

 I called my friends and allies who had helped manage the businesses in Colombia and Ecuador (by then we had already closed the Mexico business) and told them I no longer wanted to own the Latin America markets. To show my appreciation for everything they had done for me, my family, and thousands of members of the sales force, I told them I would leave the businesses in their hands. I handed over all shares of the Colombia and Ecuador businesses and left the entire remaining inventory from each country in their hands. I gave each one of them a L'eudine business as a gift. In time, those businesses succeeded and L'eudine is still active in Ecuador and Colombia, selling the same products we sold in Venezuela.

I've never been political, but I am very much a nationalist. For as long as I can remember, I've been passionate about being Venezuelan and specifically being from Maracaibo. When I gave away the businesses in Ecuador and Colombia, I opened up dreams for those people in their homelands but my Venezuelan dream was coming to a crushing end. I had already left Maracaibo when Leudin and I moved to Miami, but now I was *really* leaving. Everything I had built was gone. Venezuela gave everything to us. Everything my family and I have today, the success of MONAT — everything — is because of what we were able to do in Venezuela. In my heart I know the American Dream wouldn't have happened without the love, support, and the blessings I received in Venezuela. That set everything up.

What I learned in leaving Venezuela and taking control of B&R was that if you're not willing to go through the nightmare, you're not prepared for the dream. Success does not come without sacrifice. Sometimes when we face difficult moments in life we can say, "God, why did you punish me like this?" We don't understand that God is actually giving us the path. God is giving us everything we need to be able to reach better opportunities. When we purchased the B&R factory that was

FOR MY PEOPLE

ruined and in debt, it wasn't hard to feel like we were being punished. In moments like those, we often see life in a negative light; we view it as a punishment and often surrender. But what if instead we regard these difficult moments as opportunities to keep challenging ourselves? If we wouldn't have done that with B&R, we wouldn't have our own factory today, and we would have lost such a great opportunity with MONAT. We can see that now only because we continued on. In the moment, B&R was a nightmare. With time, it became another great business opportunity. When you are going through tough times and difficult moments, search for the positive reason. There has to be a positive — something to learn or a path that can be taken to achieve your best opportunities. It wasn't fun, but we were able to support the hits. It wasn't fun, but we were able to face the challenges. We didn't enjoy it, but fear did not defeat us. I cried the day we had to close L'eudine and leave our people behind. And I'm not embarrassed to admit that sometimes I still can't contain my emotions when I sit and reflect on those difficult days. I cry for Venezuela. I weep for Maracaibo. Thinking about Venezuela makes me emotional not only because of what I left behind but because of everything it gave me. Venezuela made me, and thanks to those lessons and that platform, the American Dream was possible.

THE COURAGE TO LEAVE

I can't explain the feeling of courage that I had to have to make the decision to leave tens of thousands of people unemployed. They were more than market partners — they were friends, and together we managed to strengthen a personal dream and turn it into a collective dream. What made me make the decision to close L'eudine was realizing there was no other choice because the people who ran Venezuela then, and still do today, wanted to destroy the country to empower themselves. There was corruption, there was inflation, there were limits on imports, and every day there was less purchasing power. I knew that if I maintained the business in Venezuela, I would still lose millions of dollars and would never be able to change those factors.

I learned valuable lessons about developing leaders and developing successful people through that experience. I was sad to leave Venezuela and nervous to tell my people that L'eudine was closing, that we couldn't go any further. But I learned that when you do things the right way, and when you support people so they can develop their skills and have the opportunity to improve their quality of life, when people feel that you are helping them to be able to change many things in their lives, the result is admiration and respect. When we had to close the business in Venezuela, there wasn't one person who criticized us or condemned the decision. They understood

FOR MY PEOPLE

what was happening in the country and they knew we wouldn't abandon them if we had any other choice. It's one of the greatest lessons I've learned: support people, be honest and fair to people, and they will respond positively. To me, that's the way I think you manage and develop the best leadership.

The year after we closed L'eudine and pursued a new business in America full time, inflation in Venezuela reached 38.5 percent. By 2015, the inflation rate in the country had surpassed 100 percent, and it was estimated that more than 5 million Venezuelans have fled the country since that year. More than half of the country sank into poverty. I returned to Venezuela occasionally during those times, but every day it became more dangerous for me to go back. When I moved to Miami, my security team stayed in Venezuela, and when I'd return to visit, I called them so they could protect me. The last time I visited Venezuela, one of them said to me, "Señor Luis, I recommend you be careful coming here. The bad people in the city already know you're coming." That comment made me think hard, and I decided not to go back.

It's not that there *was* sadness when I left Venezuela behind. There still *is* sadness. I think about the house where we lived in La Rotaria and the memories with my brothers. I would love to visit again and see my street, my neighborhood, and my friends, but especially my family.

REBEL LEADERSHIP

Nowadays, I see pictures on social media of my family meeting up on a Sunday just like we used to, and it makes me nostalgic and emotional. That was the culture of my family. We would always go to my grandparents' house, and we kept that part of our culture until the day we had to leave our home behind. Not being able to share my life with my family and with my friends and not being able to visit the land where I was born have caused a lot of frustration for me for a long time. But with time I learned that in life, you have to adapt. Back in Venezuela, in my home city of Maracaibo, we have a traditional folklike music called *gaita*. I still listen to gaita music every week here in my house in Miami. My children don't like it — they listen to Bad Bunny and such — but I love it. There is a beautiful bridge called the General Rafael Urdaneta Bridge (no relation) that connects Maracaibo and the western part of Venezuela to the rest of the country. To get to Maracaibo from the rest of Venezuela, you have to cross the bridge, and residents always said that it's because Maracaibo is a different country. It is a special place, and I'm still sad that I can't go there, not even on vacation. I still daydream about driving across that bridge to return to my homeland.

One is always going to love one's country and miss it, but just like we had to leave our country because of the crucial need, we are just as grateful to this country, the

FOR MY PEOPLE

United States, which opened its arms and gave us the opportunity to go forward. Every year when we conduct our annual financial assessment, I ask the people from the company's financial department, "How much did we pay in taxes this year?" I know this sounds crazy, but deep down it makes me happy because I feel like I'm paying back for what this country has given us and, in one way or another, thanking this country for giving us the opportunity to pursue the American Dream. Giving back to this country gives me peace of mind, knowing I contribute with the ones who have given us the opportunity and opened the doors for us. Changing the quality of life for the North American people who are part of our sales force is another way of paying it forward. It's something we feel is necessary for us to do.

Life has taught me over the years that if you do the same things, you will get the same results. When Ray and I began to look for alternatives, they would seem crazy to many, but for us, they were new opportunities to pursue our dream in America. As operations in Venezuela were winding down, we began to study the North American market. We studied successful companies in the United States — what they were doing, what premium products they had, what business plans they offered, and what markets were still undeveloped. It wasn't an easy task, but I have to thank God that Ray had prepared and studied a lot, traveling to conferences and meeting with the best in direct selling.

MONAT was born out of a need to find an alternative to our situation. Already living in Miami with no business to go back to in Venezuela, we needed to start an American business with roots and values intrinsic to its people. I reinforce what I have always said in my conferences: YOU CANNOT LET ANYONE STEAL YOUR DREAM. It's written in capital letters so that you never forget it. When we started telling people about our new dreams, many people assumed that we could not achieve them and told us we would fail. A Venezuelan man who is only a high school graduate, who doesn't know how to speak English, who has no experience in the North American market, is going to conquer the direct sales market in the United States, with so much competition? Everything was against us. But as I've told you, I am a man who believes in himself and in his talents and virtues. I am also a betting man who is not afraid of failure and will try as many times as necessary to reach the goal. I told Ray, "We are going forward, against all odds, and I'm sure we will make it." I affirm it endlessly: if you have the appropriate behaviors, the doors will open in front of you. Even if for a moment you think there is nothing left to do, you will see the light at the end of the road.

MY STORY IN PHOTOS
HERE ARE SOME OF MY FAVORITE MOMENTS IN TIME

With Leudin and my amazing team in Ecuador during a L'EUDINE Ecuador event, circa 2012.

With my children Lu, Luisana, Ray, and Javi during one of my birthday celebrations in my office, circa 2017.

With my children Javi, Lu, Luisana, and Ray during a MONAT incentive trip, circa 2018.

With my daughter Lu on stage during an emotional moment we were able to share.

With Ray, my son, friend, and business partner, circa 2013.

With my mentor and friend John C. Maxwell and my wife, Leudin, and daughters Luisana and Nicole, circa 2018.

During one of our unforgettable events for ANGEL'S, this was a special moment on stage with my father and siblings, circa 2004.

With the love of my life, Leudin, circa 2004.

My sales force in Venezuela—they are an amazing group of people, circa 2016.

Our enthusiastic sales force in Venezuela, circa 2006.

My wife, Leudin, and my daughter Luisana during a special moment, circa 2003.

My amazing allies—David Calanche, Gloria Briceño, my wife, Leudin, and Dubi and Jose Luis Piña—during an event in Venezuela, circa 2003.

I've always been passionate about distribution and logistics; here I'm giving our sales force in Venezuela a tour of our warehouse, circa 2005.

One of my best memories in Venezuela is of our offices and corporate staff, circa 2016.

Leudin, Luisana, and me during one of our FUN events, circa 2004.

Leudin and I are always happy to see our sales force enjoy our experiences and events, circa 2006.

Making sure our distribution and logistics are in great order is always a passion for me, circa 2005.

My amazing allies, my sister Yixa Urdaneta and her husband, David Briceño, at a company celebration.

My father is the one who taught me to be kind and fair, circa 2006.

Here with my brothers Leonardo, Omar, and Edixon Urdaneta and my father, Luis Urdaneta, in our house in "La Rotaria," the house where we grew up, circa 1993.

Here with my boys, Ray and Javi Urdaneta. They are two of my greatest allies, circa 2015.

A photo of the young me. My first phase of dreaming big and manifesting big dreams, circa 1980.

With my sisters, Yixa and Yenny, and brothers, Leonardo and Jesus, during a special family trip, circa 2016.

With my son and friend Ray during a business trip, circa 2017.

My joy and pride are my family. As you can see, we like to work hard and play hard, circa 2016.

With my youngest princess Nicole Urdaneta, circa 2017.

My children and I during a company event we hosted for our employees, circa 2019.

My children and the ocean—I can't love this picture enough, circa 2017.

During one of my favorite and most emotional MONAT event moments, when I was celebrating with our sales force that I had become a new US citizen.

The day I became a US citizen in 2019 was a blessed day.

My five children—they are my heart, my force, and my "why," circa 2016.

During a FEAST WITH GRATITUDE, which is one of our yearly traditions of hosting families in need to celebrate Thanksgiving. We do this every November through our MONAT GRATITUDE FOUNDATION, circa 2019.

Here are my amazing mother and father. I always admired my mother because she was a fighter, but when she told me she was going to join my Tupperware business, she became my ultimate hero, circa 1988.

My mom, EUDA FUENMAYOR— she was a winner and her mindset and attitude were indestructible. I'm the fighter and the dreamer I am because of her example, circa 1988.

My mom, Euda, was my biggest example, my inspiration, and my resilient teacher, circa 1995.

While I was having my open-heart surgery, my family (like always) stood by my side. They waited next to me the whole time, and this is the photo of them waiting for my doctor after the surgery in 2017.

A family picture during a recognition moment for my sister Yixa and her husband, David, circa 2008.

A special picture with my sisters and best friends Yixa and Yenny Urdaneta, circa 2003.

CHAPTER 12

PROJECT USA

SOON AFTER the Venezuelan business was shuttered and the Miami corporate office emptied, Ray walked into my office. There were no more product sales and our cash flow was running low, but we were still spending an exorbitant amount of cash each month to maintain the office, factory, and warehouse. For weeks, Ray and Marjorie had hinted that we needed to find ways to cut costs. Now, my son stood across my desk pleading with me.

"Dad, we're in a critical situation," Ray said. "Let's get rid of these offices. They're really expensive, and we don't know when this is going to work. Maybe we can leave the offices and we can all move to the factory. That way we save money."

We had a nice, big office in Miami that we had leased with the intent to run L'eudine Latin America. But in an office with space for thirty people, there were now only six of us. Across Miami we had a factory to maintain that wasn't producing anything, and each day our financial assets diminished as expenses increased and income dwindled. We each had an office, but the cubicles outside sat empty. It was like a ghost town. From a business standpoint, Ray and Marjorie had a point, but I couldn't accept closing the office. I felt that moving into the manufacturing plant would crush our motivation. It wasn't something I aspired to. We didn't have a business, but we had great offices, and we would dress up every day and sit in the conference room focused on coming up with our next venture — in direct sales or otherwise. The offices were inspiring. I was convinced we were going to brainstorm a great idea and succeed from there.

"Ray, we are not moving from here," I said. "We're going to start from here, regain this area, and fill the office with people who are going to help us succeed. The project we're going to do is going to work and we're going to need this space."

When Ray pushed back, I stood my ground and looked at him.

"Leave!" I said. "Get out and find some alternatives. Yes, we are losing a lot of money, but have this clear: we're not going to give up our offices. We're not closing our factory."

When Ray went back to his office and closed his door, I looked out the window and the situation hit me, and I started crying. I knew the company was at a critical

PROJECT USA

moment and I couldn't see a path to get through it. As I stood in my office alone, I continued weeping, letting everything out that I needed to release. Wiping my tears from my eyes, I started to reflect on my life, thinking, *I've already fallen a few times, and I've gotten back up again. I'm going to get back up again now and we're going to get out of this.* When I shed the feeling of powerlessness, I dried my tears and summoned the energy I knew I needed to face those challenges head on. It was a challenge that involved not only me but also my family. The decision to keep spending money on the office created great anguish, but I walked out of my office convinced that I was going to be able to start a new business. One thing I have said often is, "How many times are you going to fall to be able to reach success? Many." In my own situation, I don't know how many. I've fallen a lot. But it's important to understand that falling and failing are part of the process and that if you have the courage and the conviction to persevere, no matter how tough the situation is, you can thrive and usually overcome it. I don't say that because I heard it or read it in a book. It's because I have lived it. I've lived beautiful experiences of success but also terribly hard experiences of failure. That's the reason why I can speak about falling and say that it's true — you can get back up.

During those days I would lock myself in my office

and cry. It's important to recognize that every successful person is a human being who suffers, who feels depressed, who has fears, who has doubts, and who fights daily against all of those things. The people who are able to conquer their adversities are the ones who succeed, but it's a daily fight. I was worried, but each day when the six of us got together for lunch, I hid my fears and always projected strength. There are two important factors to staying the course. One is visualizing the things we want to change. The second is having courage. To succeed, you need to visualize your dreams and have the courage to face the situations that stand in your way.

When most people fall to the ground, it breaks their spirit and they run away. Why? Because most people justify their failures with external reasons. I knew that my fear was an external enemy. I had to remain where I needed to be. I had to correct something inside of me to get things to change. That's when I told myself that I would stand my ground and not detour off the path to my dream. I told Ray we would keep the offices open, and I didn't really know if those cubicles would ever be occupied again. But I knew we needed the offices more than ever because it was going to push us to make big things. We didn't know what the big thing was that we were going to do. We were just trying to survive at that point, but we had a dream of creating a new direct sales company in North America.

PROJECT USA

There's a big difference between the one who is dreaming and believes it and the one who dreams it and doesn't believe it. There are dreams with action and there are dreams without action. I've always believed that. Success is a matter of dreaming, believing in your dream, and having the conviction that you will make it with the appropriate actions. We didn't have a company, a product, or a name. But we had an office, and we showed up each day focused on one thing: Project USA. We sat in the conference room day after day determined that somehow, some way, we were going to open our own direct sales company in the United States.

DARE TO DREAM BIG

For many months, Project USA felt like a lesson in stagnation. We were surviving thanks to our savings and also because L'eudin Ecuador was profitable, which helped to support all the expenses in Miami.

Our wheels were spinning as we sat in the conference room throwing out ideas, but we were going nowhere. From the beginning we were convinced that the direct sales system and strategy held the most power, but we lacked the crucial element: a strong product. With that, we were confident we could achieve positive results. The question was, what was the product?

REBEL LEADERSHIP

As Ray traveled to direct sales conferences across the United States and studied the country's market, we saw just how many direct sales companies there were. We had built a $200 million company in Venezuela with L'eudine, and we wondered if our direct sales company could be that big in America. It was an established market and there was low employment need like there had been in the emerging Latin America markets. We needed a new business, but in those early days there were creeping doubts about whether or not we would end up back in direct sales.

Those doubts began to subside one day when Ray returned to the office after attending a direct sales convention in Dallas. He was excited and motivated by what he had seen and heard there. "It's crazy," he said. "This is what we need to do." Ray handed me a copy of the *Direct Selling News* magazine he had picked up, which contained a breakdown of the top five hundred direct sales companies. As I flipped through the pages, I saw four direct sales companies that had been around for only three or four years and were already selling $300 million or more each year. For the first time in months, I felt excited about the prospect of returning to the direct sales business, this time in America. "This is the business. In three or four years we could be selling the same," I told Ray. "Now let's find the product."

PROJECT USA

The safest path into the direct sales market was wellness consumables. Most of the companies at the top of the rankings in that magazine were selling wellness products — protein shakes, bars, and other consumable products. A few companies were a study of success. The wellness consumables company had opened its doors in 2005 and by 2013 had surpassed $500 million in sales. Some of these successful companies were exploding at the time. Like everybody else, we explored ideas for wellness consumables, but we couldn't hit on a concept that would set us apart in the market. We were eager to return to direct sales but stumped on how.

"What should we sell?" was the constant question. We sat around the conference table for hours thinking about what we could do. We owned a factory. "What could we do with B&R?" we thought. Several months into Project USA, one of Ray's employees, Jesus, approached him. "Ray," he said, "why don't we work on hair?" One of B&R's specialties was haircare products, which was was a top-seller category at L'eudine. Ray looked at this data and trend at B&R and we decided to move forward with the idea. Furthermore, Jesus had an idea to differentiate a shampoo product. "You know what's a good trend is anti-aging for hair," he said. Ray understood that to start a direct sales company the product needed to be a conversation starter. At that time, hardly anybody was thinking about the aging of his or her hair. Ray started going up to people and asking them if they knew how the age of their hair changed in their twenties and thirties and forties. *This is good*, he thought. Then he realized that inside the direct selling industry there were no companies focused on this category. That's when he came to me with the idea. "I think hair is a good idea," he told me. At first, I wasn't convinced. "Why shampoo?" I asked. Ray showed me the magazine again. "It's really simple, Dad," he said. "There is not one company in the direct sales industry that has this anti-aging haircare focus." Ray has always had strong business instincts and he presented a convincing plan. He had gone to CVS and Walgreens and noticed the drugstores were selling some high-quality shampoos for $30. *If CVS and Walgreens are doing it*, he thought, *it's because there's a market*. Ray researched that there was $87 billion spent on haircare products every year in the United States. It seemed like a good opportunity. I saw Ray and the team were excited. I didn't doubt it for long. I said yes. We had a product.

To achieve results, we knew we had to have a quality shampoo that worked. To do that, it would be a costly product. When Ray went to a CVS store to research the shampoos, he saw that while there were a few premium

PROJECT USA

shampoos, some of the shampoos sold for as little as $6. To be able to make the quality product we wanted to have, we estimated that we would have to sell it at premium prices. That was an enormous difference. Tupperware is plastic containers, and in Venezuela, plastic products are sold at supermarkets for as little as $1. If you wanted a Tupperware container, it cost $12, but people bought it. It's possible to sell a good, high-quality product.

Initially, we looked at creating an all-natural haircare product that could compete with the regular brands. We started working with the research and development team at B&R to create something modern and natural. The chain of events that led to the new business was a blessing from God. If the L'eudine business hadn't folded, we would have still been in Venezuela. But it did, we came to the United States in pursuit of Project USA, and then B&R fell into our hands because of a rough financial situation. Sometimes problems happen to you and you wonder, *Why is this happening to me?* We didn't realize at the time that the collapse of B&R would turn out well. But because we owned B&R, our pursuit was always in tandem with finding a way to pair the two. If we didn't have B&R, who knows which other manufacturer we would have looked for and what product we would have settled on. Together with B&R we created a company for the twenty-first century using the same foundations they had learned through years of experience developing cosmetics products. Through a long process, we created a signature formula called REJUVENIQE® Oil Intensive, which would be the foundation of all of our products. This formula promised to work against the damaging effects of sun, the environment, product use, chemical processes, and aging to provide both instant and long-term benefits for hair. We were convinced we had a haircare line that could set itself apart.

When we settled on the idea of marketing haircare, it was a big risk. There were very few direct sales companies selling haircare products. There were two ways of thinking: either it was a great idea because no one had done it or it was a really, really bad idea because no one had done it. We didn't take the safe path. That would have been with what we knew with lotions or mists or what everybody else was doing with shakes and bars. We went with the bet, with the gamble that it might be really great or it might end very badly. Life is a gamble. The ones who risk less win less. And the ones who risk more win more. The ones who are fearful will rarely reach their dreams. The ones who dare are the ones who reach the top. We were all in on hair. We were focused on finding people to join our family so we could all make the American Dream together.

PROJECT USA

FROM SO GOOD TO MONAT

Project USA began in earnest in 2013 with the goal of launching the company in the summer of 2014. By early 2014 we were making progress — we finally had a product to work on — but we still didn't know what the company was going to be named and we still needed someone to guide us into the North American market.

I had been in direct sales since I attended that first Tupperware meeting in 1982 and had mastered virtually every aspect of the business, from going door-to-door and holding meetings as a member of the sales force, to running my own market in Maracaibo as a distributor, to managing the corporate office. My team knew how to manage a direct sales business to great success, but we also understood that the connection with Hispanic people was not going to simply translate to the same connection with the people in North America. Direct sales is direct sales, but there are distinct cultural differences. The first impression of whatever Project USA would become was crucial, and we wanted to launch the company with somebody at the forefront who would connect us in the best way with the United States market.

Our search for a North American consultant began with Ray literally searching terms such as *direct sales consultant* on Google. After a while, he didn't come up with anything, so he tried LinkedIn. After researching thoroughly, he came across a woman named Debbie Squier who was a recruiter of talent for direct sales companies. It seemed like the perfect match, so Ray sent a message. "Hey, can you help recruit someone for me?" he wrote. "I need a president for the direct sales company we're launching." As our luck had it, Debbie had something better to offer. "I do that," she said. "But actually, my husband is a retired direct sales executive. If you want, we can come to your office and you can consult with him. I can help you recruit talent, but he can give you advice in other areas." That's how we met Stuart MacMillan, who had helped grow Arbonne International, the direct sales company specializing in cosmetics and skincare.

Stuart and Debbie flew to Miami to advise us and help search for talent to launch the still-nameless company. We began hiring people across divisions but still couldn't find a president. At one point, I offered the role to a friend who had been in the United States for a long time and spoke English. I explained the business plan and told him I wanted him to be our partner. He would earn half of what he was earning at his current job, but we also offered him 10 percent of the company on top of his salary. But he wasn't interested in the project as it was only a vision and we were building everything from zero. He said, "No thanks." He turned us down.

PROJECT USA

Meanwhile, Stuart kept paying attention to what we were saying in our strategy meetings. One day he stopped us. "Why search for a president?" he said. "Let's stop searching. I offer myself to be the person who helps you." Throughout the process, Ray and I had been keeping an eye on Stuart, but he was retired so we assumed he wasn't interested. When he suggested himself for the position, Ray and I recognized the opportunity. Stuart came out of his retirement and started working with us.

Slowly but surely, Project USA was becoming a reality. But as we inched closer to our launch date goal, we faced a massive problem: we couldn't come up with a name! Finding a name for the company was a nightmare. By then, the company had grown to ten employees, and at one point all of us met in the conference room day after day for ten consecutive days in search of a name. We wrote down thousands of letter combinations, names, phrases, and words. One was worse than the next. After all those days sitting around the conference room table, we still couldn't come up with a cool name. Burned out, we finally hired a creative agency. When they came into the office, they blew us away with the presentation. We were tired, and because the presentation was so cool, we agreed it was great. Ray and Lu were ecstatic. They left the room and called

Stuart, who hadn't yet moved to Miami.

"Stuart, we're so excited," they told him. "We found the name."

"Oh, my gosh!" he said. "What's the name?"

"It's *So Good*," they told him.

There was a pause.

"*So Good*," he repeated. "So it's not great."

The agency had left the office only five minutes earlier. Everybody in the office had been celebrating. We finally had a name to launch the company! Stuart's muttered words, "So it's not great" deflated us like the air being let out of a balloon. *Oh, my gosh*, Lu and Ray thought, *we don't have a name*.

As far as I knew, *So Good* was the new name of the company. But after hanging up with Stuart, Lu was scrambling behind the scenes. She went to our creative director, Ana's, office. Everything was ready except for the name. "We need to lock down inside of the conference room," Ana told her. "We need to have a name, because if not, we're not going to launch." The two went to the conference room and called in another employee, Frances. "Today," Lu said, "the only thing we're going to do is find a name." All of the words that the team had put together were still up on the boards. They started playing with the words and giving grades to each one. At the end, the two highest-ranked words

PROJECT USA

among the three of them were *modern* and *nature*. *Modern* represented the technology of both B&R's manufacturing and our formulas. *Nature* received a high ranking because we wanted to have naturally based ingredients.

It was a magical light bulb moment. "What if we combine the words?" they wondered. "Oh, it would be *MO* from *modern* and *NAT* from *nature*." They started googling and the word didn't exist. Ray and I are visual people so Lu instructed Ana to create a logo to present to us. "No, no, no," Ana said. "We need approval right now!" Just then, Ray was walking past the conference room. "Ray, come into the conference room!" They showed him the new name: *MONAT*.

"That's weird," he said. "How do you pronounce it?"

"We need to move forward," Lu insisted.

"OK, I like it," he said. "Let's move forward."

My children know I hate being indecisive. I hate indecision. As far as I knew, we had chosen *So Good* as the new name. When Lu came into my office and told me she was going to change the name, I was angry. "No, no, no!" I said. "You're not going to change the name again. That's enough." But after coming up with MONAT, Lu and her team created a logo and called me into the conference room. I remember walking in and seeing the logo. "I like it," I told them. We had gone so many weeks looking

REBEL LEADERSHIP

at words and going back and forth. The only thing waiting was the name, and now we had it. Everything was by God's design. He guided us through everything and was able to put everything together perfectly.

That's how it happened. A miracle called MONAT was born.

CHAPTER 13

THE AMERICAN DREAM

LIFE TEACHES us that dreaming doesn't cost anything. From the time I lived with my family in our home with clay walls and sand floors on the outskirts of Maracaibo, I have always been a dreamer. Perhaps it was because in those formative years, that's all I could do. Those dreams carried me to a life filled with ambitious goals that sometimes only I could see.

As it became clear that Project USA was going to be a reality, we hired staff with experience in the United States. When the regional sales managers were hired, even they were taking a risk by leaving behind careers in other established direct sales companies to come latching on to our dream. The company had a strategy with grand ambitions, but at that time it still wasn't fully realized. As we sat around the conference table at one of our first meetings, I laid out my lofty sales projections for the first year, evoking laughter from the sales staff. "That doesn't make any sense," one of them said. "You won't be able to accomplish that." So I asked, "What is your projection for the first month of sales?" "Fifty thousand the first month," I remember him saying. I was frustrated.

"You're crazy," I said.

I turned to Ray to vent, reverting to Spanish. They saw the expression on my face and could tell I was arguing.

"If it's fifty thousand dollars, then we are wasting our time," I adamantly told Ray to tell everyone in English. "Four hundred thousand dollars minimum."

When Ray and I first started planning Project USA in 2013, we set an ambitious goal of launching the company in summer 2014. By June 2014, we still had nothing and nobody. The common belief in direct sales is that you need five hundred distributors in the first year to have a successful business. We still needed *one*. We hired the regional managers to assist with the recruiting process, but as the summer continued we were getting close to the launch and still had no distributor leads. A friend suggested to us that we run a campaign on Facebook to find leads. "Maybe you could do an advertising campaign on Facebook," they suggested. We put together a web page and launched a $5,000 advertising campaign on the social media platform in July 2014. With

THE AMERICAN DREAM

that one campaign, we started getting people to sign up as distributors or, as we refer to them now at MONAT, market partners. The second referral from that campaign was a woman named Toni Vanschoyck, who came from another direct sales company to sell for us as a market partner. She started making calls, and that led to the next person and the next and the next. In time, Toni became the first MONAT market partner to reach $1 million in sales, and she later became a member of MONAT's $10 million club.

By fall 2014, we brought an initial group of eleven market partners — known as the Miami 11 — to the office in Miami. They earned that trip based on a challenge we had previously launched during the prelaunch to meet with the corporate team and lay out our vision. We didn't have samples. We didn't have a website. We didn't have marketing materials. MONAT was all based on a vision. But this early group of market partners dared to believe in our dream. I remember talking to Toni after the first day at the office. "Toni," I asked, "what do you want from this business?" I'll never forget her response. "Dude," she told me, "I just want to pay my house payment." Yes, she called me "dude!" What stands out to me as I think back on that conversation is that no matter how different we were, we were also very similar. Just like my "why" to get into direct sales in 1982 was predicated on getting out of a life of financial mediocrity, Toni had a "why" to improve her place in life. I can't say it enough: you always have to have a "why" and many "whys" in your life. The initial Miami 11 shared that. They believed in our collective dream of what MONAT could become and they dared to do it because they saw the possibilities it offered to achieve their own dreams.

What helped get MONAT off the ground was a combination of that digital campaign, which brought in people like Toni, and the launch of our Founder's Club. Ray and I had done a similar concept to launch L'eudine to great success, and it worked in Venezuela. We thought a similar idea could help build interest in MONAT in the United States market. The idea behind the Founder's Club was to reward the people who shared our vision and took a chance on MONAT to jump-start the company. We told every person who agreed to become a market partner in our first twelve months of business that they would join a pool of "founders" and would receive profit-sharing from the company for the remainder of their time with MONAT so long as they maintained a certain compensation level. Our thinking was that while we knew we had a strong hair product, we also knew that the foundation of our company was going to be its people. We wanted to share the benefit with people who not only shared our vision but also helped us fight for it from the beginning.

THE AMERICAN DREAM

The offer attracted hundreds of people in the beginning because they wanted to become what were essentially business partners. The way the Founder's Club worked was that the market partners who joined at the beginning had one year to reach a certain compensation level to qualify. Depending on the rank they achieved, they received one, two, or three profit shares paid out quarterly from MONAT's Founders Pool. We benefited from the growth in the sales force in the early days, and the people who joined us benefited in the long term. Hundreds of people qualified for the Founder's Club by the end of the first year, and some of the earliest market partners who remained with the company still earn as much as $35,000 per quarter.

By the end of September 2014, through a combination of our Facebook advertising campaign and the launch of the Founder's Club, we had reached almost five hundred market partners in the prelaunch of the company. We were ready to go live. Lu put together a small party in Wynwood, a new and trendy area in Miami at that time, and we brought in the Miami 11 group the day before for them to see our offices and manufacturing plant.

It was hurricane season in Miami, and we had a huge storm that day, but we still had a great time. On October 1, 2014, MONAT was officially launched as a direct sales company in the United States market. There was a lot of work ahead, but the first part of our longtime American Dream was a reality.

The company was profitable from the beginning. By the end of the first month, we had made $350,000 from sales — just short of my bold proclamation but well above anybody else's wildest projections. But while MONAT was profitable, $350,000 was a long way from the $200 million L'eudine had netted in its peak and still wasn't nearly enough to help fund our aspirational goals. To build the business, it was critical that we travel around the United States for relationship- and community-building events. We planned incentive trips for the market partners. From the beginning there were financial challenges. I had capital, but it wasn't a lot of money. Between paying back debts from B&R, closing L'eudine, and launching MONAT, I had only so long before the money would dry up. In early 2015, only a few months removed from MONAT's launch, Ray and I searched for alternatives to get a line of credit. The problem was, there really weren't any alternatives. The banks were unwilling to extend a loan for a new company with no credit history. We faced a lot of uncertainty whether we were going to have the financial support to build the business and continue long term. By March 2016, we were almost out of capital. "Ray, we only have two months to continue financing the company," I said. "I have no more money left." I remember telling Ray,

THE AMERICAN DREAM

"I don't owe my home to anybody. Let's find a loan officer who can give us some financial assistance, even if it's at high interest." Luckily, as we began discussions about taking out a loan against my Miami home, MONAT's sales began increasing significantly. In the next two months, the magic of sales appeared and MONAT began bringing in the financial capital and cash flow necessary to support our investments.

There wasn't one particular move we made that led to the surge in sales some seven months into our venture around April 2016. Looking back, it was a culmination of many things. From the very beginning we knew the importance of getting out across the United States to spread the word about MONAT and build relationships. We were entering an entirely new market — including both haircare and a new country — and we understood we couldn't sit back and hope or wait for people to come to us. Some thirty years earlier I had gotten my start in direct sales from going neighborhood to neighborhood knocking on doors. Times were a little different, but the idea was the same. We invested a lot of money to travel across the country, from Nashville to Dallas, conducting what we called road shows. It was crucial for us to visit a number of cities and organize meetings. We weren't simply selling the idea of a new haircare product — we were selling the opportunity of the business. In the first months, the events began drawing 150, sometimes even 300 people.

To attract people to the meetings, we would rent space in a restaurant or bar and tell them to come share nice wine with us and hear about the MONAT opportunity. It was a lot different than what we had done in Venezuela. One of the first events we did was in Nashville, where we had an open bar two hours before the event started. I remember when I walked in for the meeting all of the women were a little too happy. "Ray, I'm not sure about this" I said. "I don't know if I agree with this concept." After showcasing our shampoo product, we had a renowned network marketing keynote speaker share her secrets to succeeding in the direct sales business. At the end, she called up a woman named Mandi Schmidt from the audience to talk on the stage. We learned some lessons from those first events, but the reality was, it worked. Those meetings — where we not only showcased MONAT but more importantly built connections and developed skills — were the key to getting our first market partners, who became leaders. Within a few years, Mandi was the first market partner that left her job to do MONAT full time, and she became one of the top five MONAT directors in the entire country. She became an unconditional ally.

The boost in sales that kept the company alive as we moved toward MONAT's first anniversary, in my

THE AMERICAN DREAM

estimation, was in large part due to the relationships we cultivated as we traveled around the country. As we brought on market partners, they would go out and build their teams. I don't know that there was anything special about the uptick in sales around the seventh month that kept MONAT alive. It just so happened to be when the efforts of the team in Miami to build a network, the impact of an amazing haircare line, and the hard work of our first market partners in the field began to hit their collective stride. By the end of the first year in business, it was clear that MONAT had been a viable dream. It was not only the American Dream but it became the dream I always had, which was to join my children on a project like MONAT.

For all my life I have dreamed big, but MONAT reaffirmed to me that you have to think big, whether you hit your goals or not.

TAKING THE GAMBLE

I have to confess that patience is not one of my virtues. I've never been someone who waits for things to happen. By nature I go out to search and fight for what I think belongs to me, without looking back. I don't care how much time and effort I have to put in to achieve the goal. Sometimes it's hard to wait. With no experience in the

US market, successful entrepreneurship wasn't easy and growing MONAT on my time frame was elusive.

With impatience comes the inability to stay calm and concentrate on daily life activities. No matter how much we try to advance scenarios in life, God's timing is exact. When you try to jump to the finish line, it's easy to miss critical steps along the way, and oftentimes impatience with our goals and dreams only derails us. In many cases our lack of patience generates desperation and we lose peace of mind. You feel tied hand and foot, not knowing what to do next. I thank God for having the best partners in the world — Leudin, my son Ray, and his siblings — who, with wisdom and patience, calmed me down and lowered anxiety levels caused by my lack of patience. Impatience can block you and paralyze you. This is the worst thing that can happen to a leader because leaders must be ready to act at all times. Impatience has often generated in me a state of strong anguish, causing the wait for the triumph to become a torture that I endure daily. The reality is, this behavior is harmful, and many times it ruins our plans and delays us on the road to our goals. I know what it feels like to fight for your goals and yearn for your dreams. But I've learned from moments of self-inflicted anxiety that we can't skip the process. At some point in your life you've probably been told something similar to this famous phrase by Zig Ziglar:

THE AMERICAN DREAM

"Success is not a destination, it's a journey." I know that probably just sounds like another motivational pitch, but I'm telling you it's true. My entire life I've fought against impatience. It can be a constant battle to fend off impatience and enjoy the moments.

By the end of 2015, MONAT's first full year in business, the company had reached $18 million in total sales. We were growing, but it wasn't like we were swimming in cash. By the time we paid for the products, paid commissions to market partners, reinvested in B&R, and so on, there wasn't a lot of money available. We were counting every dollar that was coming in and trying to determine how we could grow. The profits we had were small compared to all of the bills we had monthly. I was feeling a strong, anguishing impatience by late 2016. What's interesting about impatience is that while it can be harmful when we allow it to derail us from our journey to success, a little impatience can actually be a good thing. When impatience makes you give up on your dreams or quit too soon — for example, leaving a job because it's taking too long to get the promotion you dream of — it can be harmful. Impatience born out of the desire to reach our goals faster or to take shortcuts to reach a destination or reduce the sacrifice required to achieve becomes distracting and is detrimental to where you want to go. But there is a fine line that comes with impatience. You see, I found that some impatience isn't inherently bad. Sometimes, a bit of impatience can motivate us to keep going; it keeps us from becoming complacent. Everybody gets stuck in life. Impatience, when used as a boost to find alternatives and stay the course, can be the push we need to keep going. So patience is not always a virtue. Patience without action is simply waiting. Impatience can sometimes be the push we need to act and take calculated risks.

THE WORD BEGINS TO SPREAD

When Ray was born in 1981, I was getting ready to start my career in direct sales at Tupperware. He was roughly twelve months old when I started knocking on doors around Maracaibo, and there was one moment in particular that left a lasting impression on me and still guides me today. Tupperware would create challenges for the salespeople, and the winners would have the opportunity to pick out a gift for their children. The most valuable things were the trips I won. Even before I had anything, it gave me the opportunity to earn a prize that I could enjoy with Ray. I learned from Tupperware the importance and value of having a human connection, and I practice it at all levels of business. That human touch, in my opinion, is the key to success and longevity.

THE AMERICAN DREAM

That principle is what guided us to invest millions of dollars in events and unforgettable experiences, to recruit and develop market partners, and later plan annual trips to places such as Las Vegas, the Dominican Republic, and The Bahamas. Those millions of dollars are an investment in our people, creating a connection that has allowed us to build a sales force and maintain a business. Direct sales is not simply about having a great product; it's a relationship business.

MONAT finished 2016 with 12,000 market partners and saw total sales jump from $18 million in 2015 to $41 million in 2016. By the end of January 2017, it was clear our efforts were gaining traction. Between launching the MONAT Motor Club, which allowed top-performing market partners to qualify for any model white Cadillac, and our other promotions and rewards, the company reached $4 million in January sales alone. It was the beginning of one of the most amazing years in direct sales. By November 2017, MONAT was doing $40 million in monthly sales, a 1,000 percent increase from January. By the end of 2017, MONAT was the No. 1 premium haircare company in the world by total revenue, reaching $314 million in sales. In the course of one year, the company had gone from 12,000 market partners to 150,000 market partners. The growth from $41 million to $314 million was a staggering 667 percent, earning MONAT *Direct Selling*

News' BRAVO Growth Award for the highest growth of any direct selling company in the industry from 2016 to 2017. Word about MONAT began to spread around the direct sales industry because of the company's hyper growth. From the beginning we had set out to build a direct sales company for the twenty-first century that focused not only on market partners but also on end customers who purchased our shampoo and other products from them. By the end of its third year, through a combination of technology, social marketing, and an investment in relationships, MONAT was finally realizing its potential. In addition to the more than 150,000 market partners, the company also had 450,000 end customers.

We always say that market partners are going to come to MONAT searching for opportunities and their love for the products, and that they're going to start in the business of direct sales searching for an opportunity to earn more. But afterward, money will become secondary when they are given the opportunity to grow and build human connections. There is nothing as powerful as recognizing people and giving them value. Recognizing and valuing people doesn't just give you happy people, it also gives you the opportunity of having loyalty and longevity. There were times where other businesses would offer my leaders more money to go with them, but they wouldn't leave because of the recognition and

THE AMERICAN DREAM

the value they received in our company. I have a lot of faults. I don't run the perfect business. But I truthfully believe in recognizing and valuing people when they deserve it because I know how important it was for me at Tupperware.

When I was in Venezuela, I had employees who stayed with me for more than fifteen years. Marjorie started with me at Tupperware, and when I was starting my own business I went back for her. It wasn't easy to convince her, but I managed to do it, and it's satisfying knowing that she agreed to come with me. After so many years, she's the financial leader and the consultant who we always ask for advice with numbers at ALCORA and, of course, MONAT. Kathy, who finally left to start her own business, was with me for more than twenty years. She started as a sales analyst and ended up becoming the analyst for the entire company. I met Veronica when she was a bank executive and I invited her into direct sales, where she developed in the business and became a top distributor every step of the way, from Tupperware to SwissJust to Angels to L'eudine. The same thing happened with Dubi and Jose Luis. I offered all three of them a percentage of the L'eudine business to come with me on my dream, and working hand in hand we achieved that. Loyalty and gratitude prevailed because they saw that I not only compensated them well but I also valued them as people. The longevity of all these people is based on not only paying them but respecting them, giving them value as human beings, and recognizing them.

As we began to grow, I empowered my daughter Lu with creating MONAT's recognition program. Just as Ray had helped the company master a product line, Lu helped create a recognition program that remains the core of everything I believe. I still remember the first time my name was mentioned as a top salesperson in Tupperware and when I checked into the five-star hotel that Tupperware put me in. I'll never forget the trip I earned to Puerto Rico as one of the top distributors. Those moments remain with me because they made me feel valued. It made all of those sacrifices — leaving my children with their grandparents, driving twelve hours a day, knocking on doors — worth it. I was bettering my life but also being recognized for the role I was playing in helping other people improve theirs. I have always been convinced that showing people value and lifting their self-esteem helps for retention.

We invested a lot of time and millions of dollars to recognize market partners and leaders. With Lu's efforts, we began sending market partners flowers on their birthday and Mother's Day or Father's Day. When they reached a certain rank, we would give them a suitcase.

THE AMERICAN DREAM

Eventually, we launched MONATions, where thousands of market partners get together every year to meet each other, develop as leaders, and, most importantly, be recognized. As we created the idea for MONATions, that was the most critical aspect. Whether it added thirty minutes or an hour, I wanted our deserving market partners to have their moment of recognition on the stage. I remembered what it was like to have my moment and I wanted to create that same magic, unforgettable moment for someone else. Some of my biggest frustrations through the years have come when I feel like people aren't getting the recognition they deserve. People sometimes ask, "Why do we have to do recognitions at every single event?" My answer is simple: "Because it's unforgettable for the people who are getting the recognition." And for the people watching, it inspires them to dream of the same milestone.

When we first came to the United States, there were people who told me that I wasn't going to be able to connect with North Americans because I didn't speak English. But I've always said that there is something that is universal in humans — when you give love, when you give support, when you give people affection, and when you help people change their quality of life, people will eventually value and appreciate you. It's not about communicating in one language or another. I might not have been able to communicate in the same language, but we could communicate with our expressions and with our eyes. It's beautiful to receive that type of affection with gestures. Sometimes, I think, it might even be stronger than words. When you speak with your heart, you get through. When you try to reinvent yourself, your connection doesn't exist. That's why I always say to my children, "Be who you are and speak with your soul. That is going to truly make a real connection."

Creating success stories has been one of the most important keys to reaching success in direct sales. This is what I've practiced, what I continue practicing, and what I continue telling my children. We are going to continue being successful as long as we make successful people, as long as we continue showing our people value, as long as we don't see them as an instrument to earn money but as human beings who are working with us to be able to change their quality of life.

When the direct sales industry started, it worked with that concept, and that's why it's been working for so many years. But with the passing of time, I've noticed that the concept of recognizing people's worth has been lost in many companies. Now in many cases I see that it's all about money. You can see in the leaders of the industry that what they're searching for is money, and I think that's a mistake. You have to continue producing human

THE AMERICAN DREAM

beings who are successful. You have to continue giving people value. When we opened our new corporate office in Miami in 2022, we returned to our roots. Throughout the building there are hallways filled with photographs of all members of the $1 million club, $5 million club, $10 million club, and the MONAT Motor Club. When people walk into our main corridor they will see the names and photos of the people who helped make MONAT what it is today.

What for many detractors was almost impossible — to conquer the American market — became a reality. Against many predictions, success arrived at MONAT's door. The struggle to achieve our goals, with the appropriate actions and a great team, paid off. By the end of 2017, MONAT had not only reached $314 million in sales and become the fastest-growing direct sales company but had also earned another distinction. The next spring MONAT debuted on the *Direct Selling News* Global 100 list at #52. Three years after launch, we were now among the very companies that had inspired us to chase the American Dream.

CHAPTER 14

THE POWER OF EMPOWERMENT

"SON, I WANT TO START a business and I want you to help me," I remember telling Ray over the phone in 2001 when I made the decision to start my own direct sales company. "You're going to search for the products and the tools that we need." Ray was nineteen years old, and I decided to put him in charge because I believed in him and his potential. But it wasn't just that. Ray has always been focused and responsible, and from the time he moved to America at eighteen years old, he was responsible for doing what needed to be done. Since I was familiar with his character and knew he was responsible, I took a leap of faith to put him in charge of purchasing products in the United States while I was a long-distance call away in Venezuela.

At the beginning I gave Ray some big responsibilities

— finding a manufacturing partner and researching a viable product — and monitored everything that he did. Every day he improved. He took care of the innovation of the products without knowing a lot about them, he handled the shipping from Miami to Maracaibo, Venezuela, and he worked from the garage in his house to provide us with whatever we needed. He created one product after the other and completed one project after the next, which boosted my confidence that he was the person who could help us thrive. By the time he was twenty-two, Ray was already handling the administration of the business and managing million-dollar budgets. I remember telling Ray, "I trust that you're going to do things well." I've always thought that giving people responsibility and showing confidence that they can finish the job is crucial. Whether I was consciously thinking about it then or not, that was one of my biggest lessons in empowerment.

I had to be pushed to complete high school, but while I never liked studying school subjects, I have always enjoyed learning about success stories. My friend Jose Luis Oropeza gave me a book written by John C. Maxwell in the 1980s when I started in direct sales, and I liked it because it was easy to understand and the messages were powerful. I still have a number of Maxwell books on my office bookshelf. One of them; *The 21 Irrefutable Laws*

THE POWER OF EMPOWERMENT

of Leadership, is filled with highlights and notes that I have scribbled all over the pages. One of Maxwell's laws of leadership is the Law of Empowerment. He writes,
> To lead well you need to share your power, especially with other leaders. If you give people responsibility, authority, and resources, and help them develop as leaders, they'll achieve. Believe in people, because when you, as a leader, believe in them, they'll believe in themselves.

I learned early on that a leader has to be willing to delegate. You need to take the risk of believing that other people can achieve what you did and empower them to believe in themselves. Often, when someone already has success and money, what they crave the most is power. I've tried to avoid getting stuck wanting to have that power. I fight in order to achieve that. When I wanted to do my first national convention in Venezuela, I gave Lu a $1 million budget to put together a spectacular event. Lu told me recently, "I can't believe you gave me that responsibility. I don't know if I would give a twenty-year-old that responsibility." Because of my experiences, I knew that if I was able to get there at twenty years old, I had to understand that many other people could do that too. That's why I always delegated responsibilities to people, even when they didn't have much experience. Where would

REBEL LEADERSHIP

I have ended up had Orlando not given me the chance to become a distributor in Maracaibo when I was just twenty-three? What if he had stuck to his gut and told me that I didn't have the experience for such a great responsibility? You have to bet on the people you have around you because in the end, your business depends on more than just you. That's why there are some companies that have one leader and when that leader dies, the company dies with them.

I gave Ray the opportunity of doing what needed to be done, understanding that he had the maturity to do it. He became the absolute leader of the products and boosted the business in Venezuela to the point where today at MONAT I don't even look at new products to approve them. Ray tells me there's a new product and I say, "If Ray says it's good, that's fine." I've continued to empower others, such as Javier, Lu, Luisana, Maria Castellon, Marjorie, Kathy, Stuart, and many more. To me, the key is looking for eager people, regardless of age. When we purchased the B&R factory and warehouse, we had nobody to manage the factory. We sat down as a staff and decided, "Why don't we take Maria Castellon over there?" Maria was working on the administrative side. She was responsible, she worked hard, and she had our trust. "Let's give her the opportunity," we decided. When we gave her the opportunity, Maria was sixty-three.

THE POWER OF EMPOWERMENT

She was managing the purchasing department, but we looked at the qualities we needed and placed her there temporarily to see what happened. Today, if I were asked to identify the five best leaders of the company, Maria Castellon would be among them. She had the passion, love, and focus — and she succeeded. I want to highlight an important lesson in this: the people who have experience and talent sometimes fail more than the ones who don't have experience but have the passion and focus.

Empowering people doesn't just mean giving them responsibility. Instead, empowerment is a two-way street built on trust where you give someone responsibility and in return take on risk that they might fail but that you will support them when they do. When you empower someone, they have to know that you believe in them and that you will support them when they inevitably make a mistake. Failure is part of the process and it's a risk leaders must be willing to take to empower their people. When someone feels empowered, it takes away his or her fears. When you feel empowered, you will start living the type of situations that destroy fear.

Maxwell writes later in *The 21 Irrefutable Laws of Leadership*,

> Achievement comes to someone when he is able to do great things for himself. Success comes when he empowers followers to do great things with him.

Significance comes when he develops leaders to do great things for him. But a legacy is created only when a person puts his organization into the position to do great things without him.

During the early stages of MONAT, Ray, Marjorie, Kathy, Stuart, Javi, Lu, and I were a team making up the ideas and strategies. A lot of those ideas worked and helped us achieve extraordinary results. But as time has gone on I've moved to the side little by little to empower my children and other leaders in the company. I am behind them along the way and can see the passion that my kids have for creating their own strategies. They have a pathway ahead for a very beautiful era of MONAT's future. I feel their achievements like they're my own achievements. No matter what it is in life, your project should never depend only on you. As Maxwell puts it, a good leader "pays the price today to assure success tomorrow." A good leader empowers people to dare to achieve. Today I'm a lot like an assistant coach watching from the press box at the game. When the game gets tight I might go down, analyze the game and make suggestions, and then go back to the box to watch my team perform.

Never forget that in order to achieve success, we have to help the people around us to achieve it first. For you to be successful, make your team successful.

THE POWER OF EMPOWERMENT

LEARNING FROM MISTAKES

My children have criticized me in the past about my temperament, and I've always told them, "I know very few leaders who have achieved success with a weak temperament. And I know a lot of successful leaders who have a strong temperament." This isn't something I made up; it's the story of many successful people. I admit that I don't always put makeup on my words. I search for the raw words because sometimes, when you try to sugar-coat something, people don't always get the message.

I've read the stories of many founders — Steve Jobs at Apple, Elon Musk at Tesla — and what's predominant about all of the stories I've read is how strict they are with themselves and with their people. I've often said that a leader needs to be firm. Even if you're afraid or you make a mistake, you need to be decisive. Even if your legs are shaking whenever you're making a decision, don't show it. I'm never trying to be mean or insulting. I've seen Jobs described as rude and rough. His biographer Walter Isaacson shared this anecdote in the *Harvard Business Journal:*

> I don't think I run roughshod over people," he said, "but if something sucks, I tell people to their face. It's my job to be honest." When I pressed him on whether he could have gotten the same results while being nicer, he said perhaps so. "But it's not

REBEL LEADERSHIP

who I am," he said. "Maybe there's a better way — a gentlemen's club where we all wear ties and speak in this Brahmin language and velvet code words — but I don't know that way, because I am middle-class from California.

It's important to appreciate that Jobs's rudeness and roughness were accompanied by an ability to be inspirational. He infused Apple employees with an abiding passion to create groundbreaking products and a belief that they could accomplish what seemed impossible. And we have to judge him by the outcome. Jobs had a close-knit family, and so it was at Apple: His top players tended to stick around longer and be more loyal than those at other companies, including ones led by bosses who were kinder and gentler. "I've learned over the years that when you have really good people, you don't have to baby them," Jobs told me. "By expecting them to do great things, you can get them to do great things."

Maybe some of my fire comes from our close-knit family at MONAT. Ray, Lu, and Javier are literally family, and people such as Marjorie, Kathy, and Stuart might as well be. One of the reasons I've always been straightforward with people is that I've found that many times they will come to you after they've made a mistake and tell you it happened because they didn't understand what you

THE POWER OF EMPOWERMENT

were trying to tell them. To avoid this, I'd rather explain things as clearly and plainly as possible. Sometimes my kids tell me that it's harsh, but there are times when you have to say, "It has to be done like this. Period." The point is you fail, you see your failure, and then you identify it. If you fail and you don't identify your failure, you will never learn from it. But if you fail and you understand what went wrong and accept it, then you will be able to find a way to improve on it the next time. I don't have a problem with failing — I've failed time and time again — but I don't have time for people who justify their failures. I'm conscious that we're going to make mistakes. But we will also do a lot of positive things, and if a strategy doesn't work then that doesn't have to affect you or make you feel bad, especially when you accept that it was a mistake and you learn from it. Failures are part of the process that we are living through. What I cannot tolerate is justification or excuses. I want the person who acknowledges the mistake, reflects on it, and says, "What am I going to do tomorrow to have better results?"

From the time Kathy joined me in Venezuela in 2001, she was a rock star. After starting as a sales analyst in our first business, I empowered her to become an analyst for the entire company and delegated important projects to her. For as long as I can remember, she always achieved great results. Until one day she failed for the first time. It was December, and Kathy was in charge of ILLUSION's logistics. We were selling a lot of products, but we were also doing a lot of promotions to reward the sales force. That year, one of the promotions was for Christmas toys. The sales force would sell products in November and receive their rewards in December. Because they were Christmas gifts for their children, the whole idea behind the promotion was that they were supposed to receive the rewards before Christmas. That's what they expected.

Logistically, there were a lot of complications. Everything that could go wrong did. The shipping containers with the Christmas toys arrived late from China and the United States; we couldn't find enough people to work the last two weeks before Christmas; we didn't have enough trucks to deliver the merchandise around Venezuela. The sales leaders were so desperate to get the gifts for their children that they went to our warehouse to pick up the rewards. Kathy and her team gave everything to get the gifts to the sales force, but in the end they couldn't meet their goal. Sales leaders around Venezuela were upset because when Christmas came, they didn't have gifts for their children. When Christmas ended, I called Kathy into my office.

"What's going on?" I asked. "Why is the sales force so upset?"

"We didn't get the rewards on time," Kathy said.

THE POWER OF EMPOWERMENT

"Customs didn't release the containers where the rewards came. So we were not able to give it to them on time. That's why the sales force is upset."

I asked Kathy what happened, and she started explaining all of the logistical problems she and her team had encountered.

"That sounds good in theory and it might be true," I said. "But at the end you couldn't make those results. So therefore the job was a failure."

After years of telling Kathy she was a rock star, it was the first time I told her she had failed. When I told Kathy those words, I could see how they affected her. She was ready to explode. "Let's stop talking," I said. "We will talk about this later." Kathy left the meeting crying. That night, I found out later, she went out with her friends and together they drank a whole bottle of whiskey. She was destroyed by our conversation. A few days later, I asked her to come to my office.

"How are you feeling?" I asked.

She started crying. I could tell she was mad. "I don't deserve for you to call me a failure. I worked really hard for this," she told me through tears. "I gave my soul for this, and if the rewards weren't handed out, it wasn't my fault."

"You know that is not you. The one speaking right now is your ego," I said. "I didn't call you a failure. I have not stopped trusting you. But you need to understand that in order for you to be successful in life you're going to have failures like this. You didn't get the results — that's a reality — but you got up today and you came to work to change those results. If you would have left and not come back, which was a possibility, you would have been a failure and you would have been totally defeated. But you have not been defeated, and that is the big difference."

When Kathy left the second time, we were both smiling and laughing. She came out of that meeting with the biggest lesson she could have learned that day: just because you put all of your effort into one thing doesn't mean everything is going to come out right. There is always a possibility that you will fail. That's OK! What matters is that you find a way to come up again, recognize that whatever you were trying to do didn't work, and start searching for new ways and new possibilities. Failure teaches us. The key is to accept your failure and learn from it.

CHAPTER 15

NEVER LOSE YOUR HUNGER

AFTER I TURNED fifty-seven at the end of 2018 I remember telling Lu, "When I turn sixty, I want to be a billionaire." I learned a long time ago that to continue being successful you can never settle with where you are or be content with what you have. You can be appreciative, but to continue down the path of success, you can never settle.

I've often said that you can dream big, but you don't make it to your dream without conviction and the appropriate actions. Sometimes, making your big dreams come true can be stressful, depending on how big your dream is. My biggest dream was to have a $1 billion company. And when we talked about $1 billion I was already thinking about $2 billion. My big dreams never die. People who don't constantly think about their next dream are the ones who don't accomplish the extraordinary. I believe the people who maintain the hunger of being the best every day are the ones who, in the long term, achieve the greatest results.

When we celebrated MONAT going from $4 million in sales in January 2017 to $40 million that November, there was a moment that I thought, *We made it*. But that moment didn't last long. I was already thinking about how we could go to $80 million. My biggest pleasure in life is when we go from achieving one goal to another, bigger goal. I define success and I enjoy success. But when we close a month, I always ask Ray and Marjorie, "How many sales did we have? How many leaders do we have? How many leaders gained a rank? How many hires did we make?" I always want to show our team that we can break barriers. I shared this before and I practice it all the time: don't let your hunger die, ever. The day that your hunger dies, your passion dies. And when passion dies, the urge to dream dies.

Around a year ago I said to a leader in the business, "You're earning a lot of money, but there are so many opportunities for you to multiply that as long as you keep learning and focusing on being a better leader every day. And you know what? You have the potential to launch your own business in the future." If I was only interested in the sales she could bring to me, I wouldn't have shared that message, but I told her, "Telling you this and for you

NEVER LOSE YOUR HUNGER

to achieve it will inspire others in the business to reach what you are achieving." Remember what I said about making other people successful being one of the keys to your success? I always want to search for people to be inspired to follow the path that I took, the path that I'm on, and the path that will give me opportunities to be more successful.

But what happens to so many people? They attain a little bit of success and a little bit of money and lose their focus. That is one of the titanic battles we all face. Most people, when they earn a bit of money, lose focus on what got them there. Of course, when they lose focus on those daily habits, their passion loses strength. I haven't been immune to those failings. I have seen this not only in my years at MONAT but through my lifetime and my entire experience in direct sales. I have seen people that have a few successes and then they feel powerful. They have a bit of money in the bank and they start traveling, relaxing, and enjoying themselves. And then they lose focus of what has allowed them to achieve those things. They feel successful; they think that they know everything, and stop listening, and stop learning. And if that's what money does, power is even worse. That's why I often repeat: Be careful with money. *And* be careful with power. Because if money or power dominates you, you can lose your values and lose focus on your behaviors. I've repeated it over and

REBEL LEADERSHIP

over to my kids, even recently: "Kids, don't let money and power be stronger than your values."

As I focused on developing my leadership, I realized that I didn't always need to be the main character. My first experience of "letting go" in business came when I stumbled down that ski slope in Colorado and had no choice but to leave the business in Venezuela in the hands of my team. I always believed in Kathy, Marjorie, Veronica, Dubi, and Jose Luis, but when I had no choice but to step back, I learned with my own experience the importance of empowerment. With MONAT, I had the intentional vision of empowering three of the most important people in the company — Ray, Lu, and Javier — to see what they were made of. Today, as CEO, Ray manages all operations in MONAT. Many times he's achieved wonderful results. Other times, he's made mistakes. But I dared to let those things happen so that he learns and can strengthen his image as a leader inside the company. I always demand more from my children. I demand them to demand more from themselves. Sometimes I show up at the office to see how they're leading and they ask me about important decisions, but at the end of the day, Ray is the one who operates and implements the company's strategies. The team, not me, is what has made MONAT a success.

When we launched MONAT, we did so with the idea

NEVER LOSE YOUR HUNGER

of delivering a quality anti-aging, naturally based haircare product to what we felt was an underserved premium haircare market. After becoming the biggest haircare company in direct sales by revenue in 2017, we couldn't rest thinking we had made it or become complacent and rely on our shampoos to keep carrying us forward. We needed to stay hungry and innovate. By the end of 2018, we reached $435 million in sales and moved to thirty-fifth on *Direct Selling News*' Top 100. Along the way, Ray and his team at B&R were thinking about MONAT's next product.

    Ray decided to bring his wife, Carolina, on board as the lead for this product development ideation and creation. Ray knew Carolina was a key player since she has always been devoted to skincare, and she is a student of ingredients and product effectiveness. Ray and Carolina, along with their team, created the innovation we needed in order to go to the next level. We announced our second product line, MONAT Skincare, at our MONATions conference on September 14, 2019.

    The move into skincare was a natural one. For five years, natural anti-aging innovation had been at the core of the company, but we were always wondering what we could do next. As we continued to refine our Rejuveniqe formula — the signature blend of more than fourteen botanical oils that we developed with B&R — it became clear that we could apply the same learnings and concepts that we brought to premium haircare to create other products, including skincare. We thought the move into skincare could be big, but we never could have anticipated what happened when we launched the eight-piece line consisting of cleansers, moisturizers, and an eye cream. Within thirty-six hours of launch, MONAT had sold a company-record $4 million worth of product, including $2 million in the first five hours alone. Within the first three weeks, we were halfway to what we felt was an aggressive 2019 forecast. After several products sold out and created a thirteen-thousand-person waiting list, we doubled production at the B&R manufacturing facility in response to the demand. That year, we ranked among the world's largest beauty manufacturers.

At the end of the first year, MONAT's skincare line had totaled more than $150 million in sales, and *Inc.* magazine named the company one of America's fastest-growing private companies. As that growth continued, we noticed that our customers were searching for lifestyle products to complement their routines. When we started Project USA, we hadn't yet found the perfect product to launch into the health consumables market, but we were starting to see a more natural fit alongside our haircare and skincare lines and felt we could fill a void in the market. Our research showed that there was still significant opportunity in the market. So Ray and his team began the search for a wellness line that could tie everything together in what we called a "360-degree approach to inner health and outer beauty." After an intense process of trial and error with our scientists, we finally settled on a wellness product line that focused on nutrition, rest, and exercise through a collection of products including an all-natural energy drink mix, a total greens superfood boost, pre- and probiotic capsules, a collagen powder, and sleep drops. Nearly a year after announcing our skincare line, we launched MONAT Wellness on September 12, 2020. We set an ambitious first-day sales goal, and twenty-four hours later we had set a new company record with $10 million in sales, nearly three times our projection and 10 percent of our $100 million first-year forecast. When the year ended, we had reached $804 million in annual revenue.

After selling $1.19 billion in our first five-plus years, we topped $800 million in just one year. The company had grown nearly forty-five-fold since our first full year in 2015. That year, MONAT reached #23 on the *Direct Selling News*' Top 100. How did we do it? It was a team effort filled with vision and long processes of research, development, and trial and error. But the real truth is that while there were quite literally some complex formulas involved (thanks to our scientists), what truly made MONAT innovate from one product line to three was

REBEL LEADERSHIP

simpler: We never stopped dreaming of what we could do next. We never settled on our successes.

When I reread John C. Maxwell's book *The 21 Irrefutable Laws of Leadership* after many years of it sitting on my bookshelf, I noticed several highlights I had made many years before. One of them was a quote Maxwell included from journalist Sydney J. Harris, who wrote, "A winner knows how much he still has to learn, even when he is considered an expert by others. A loser wants to be considered an expert by others, before he has learned enough to know how little he knows." Talent is never enough. That phrase has been true in my life. There are people in this world who are talented, but they kick the talent to the curb with their behaviors. How many talented people do you know who haven't achieved great success because they relied on talent alone to get there? Talent is not enough to reach your goals. I believe more in the people who have courage, dreams, passion, and conviction and who focus on what they truly want. I believe in the people who are daring and bold. Success depends on how you educate your mind and how you focus on reaching your objectives. After that, talent is helpful. But talent alone isn't what makes you successful.

I say that we have to learn to learn. Maxwell includes a highlight from former NBA coach Pat Riley, who wrote in

NEVER LOSE YOUR HUNGER

his book *The Winner Within: A Life Plan for Team Players*, "Complacency is the last hurdle any winner, any team must overcome before attaining potential greatness. Complacency is the 'success disease': it takes root when you're feeling good about who you are and what you've achieved." This is a great truth. Sometimes success can be our worst enemy and the biggest detriment to our future success. Often when people win, they become complacent with what they have, they stop learning, and lose focus on what they were chasing in the first place. One of the best traits any human can have is curiosity. That constant desire to learn is what keeps a fire burning. No matter how many times you might succeed, there is one thing you can't forget: to be able to continue having success you must never lose your hunger.

FINISH WHAT YOU START

I tossed back and forth in the hotel bed in downtown Atlanta when I finally realized something wasn't right, that it might be more than just a sleepless night. My chest was tight, my breath short, and my heart raced. It was September 7, 2021, the night before the start of MONAT's annual conference. Leudin called 9-1-1 and the paramedics rushed to the hotel room. When they ran their batch of tests, my blood pressure returned to normal. "Don't take me to the hospital," I said. There were a lot of expectations leading up to that conference. We were coming out of COVID-19 and had made a big investment in MONATions in the hope that people would return. But I feared that maybe people wouldn't show up. I was having a panic attack.

That wasn't the first night that the pressure from the demands I put on myself became too much to bear. There have been many times in my life that I spent the entire night thinking. Leudin will tell me, "Just go ahead and sleep." But I'll lay in bed all night thinking. Leudin jokes that every time I feel something like I did that night in Atlanta I go to a different doctor hoping to hear something else. Every doctor has told me the same thing: "Your problem is the stress." Ray told me that he wakes up in the middle of the night thinking, too, and I've thought to myself, *That's good.* I prefer a person who is always dreaming and always demanding more because I believe that in the end, they achieve more and inspire more people. Everyone makes their own decisions on how to manage their lives. I decided to manage my life under pressure and under constant demand. That is the path I chose, and I don't regret it. There are things I would have done differently, but my decisions worked for me and helped me attain success. Success is different for different people. Everyone decides the path they're going to take. I took the path of stress, and I'm conscious that I can't control it. I think there are very few people in this world who can calibrate the dream, the work, the demand, the passion and still dominate the stress. I don't know if there is such a balance. Reaching big goals comes with stress and sacrifice. You can decide what works for you, but if you don't have the passion and aren't aggressive, you might not make it. I know this is true: You cannot live a relaxed life and have big things. I honestly do not think that exists.

There are things I would have done differently. Looking back, I should have delegated more and empowered others sooner. Stress is part of having ambitions, but I realize now it can have a negative effect when it impacts your health. As I've gotten older, I have begun to look for ways to lower the pressure I put on myself. Although I can try to control my stress and emotions, I understand as I grow older that if I don't delegate, empower, or teach so others can ease the pressure on me, I will keep getting sick. I made the decision many years ago to empower those whom I consider trustworthy. I tell Ray so he can learn from what happened to me: "You need to delegate, empower, and give other people responsibilities so that pressure won't be permanently yours. Because if not, by the time you reach your fifties or sixties, what happened to me will possibly happen to you." But empowering other people doesn't mean lowering your expectations.

I remember telling Ray, "Let's talk about our expectations." As we started talking about MONAT's projections and the big expectations we had, he said, "But Dad, if we don't reach our goals, we're not going to look good." I told him, "We're going to look even worse if we don't show great expectations." There is a price to pay if you want to accomplish big dreams. There are a lot of people who aren't willing to pay that price and settle for thinking small. I've always dreamed big. I wanted a $1 billion company. Ray now practices it very well. Now his voice doesn't tremble when he says we are going to be a billion-dollar company. I go back to the law of attraction — you're going to have in you what you say, think, and believe in. The world belongs to and will always belong to the brave, not because you are born brave and it is a gift from God but because those of us who dare to fight for our dreams crown our success with persistence.

As I said, I come from very humble beginnings. My great-grandfather was poor; my grandfather was poor; my father was poor. I think it was up to me to break the chains of poverty and fight hard to get my family ahead. The good news is that the future isn't defined. If we are willing to set goals and fight for them, and we set the right course of action and stick to it, we will see results. Nothing is easy in life, and it was hard for me to understand that, but the result of my actions and determination brought me to where I am today.

Many people over the years have told me that I'm a lucky man.

If being lucky means to dream big, I am.

If being lucky is to be aggressive, I am.

If being lucky is to have appropriate behaviors and the right focus, I am.

If being lucky is to believe that everything is possible, I am.

You can learn from my mistakes, my failures, and, above all else, from my successes. I'm not the only lucky person in life. You can also achieve success, no matter your origins or what stage of life you are in at this moment. The important thing is that you have to believe it. I have no doubt that God believes in you. I ask you something: Do you believe in you? If the answer is yes, you have won the first stage. Start chasing your goals, and the doors that have closed will start to open again. I never stop dreaming, believing, and demanding more, because the day I stop dreaming, I will be dead for sure.

When I turned sixty in December 2021, I didn't have $1 billion. I failed to reach my goal. But I tried and I will keep on trying. I'm not afraid to fail. Reaching success is about permanently having a mindset that inspires and motivates you to overcome any of the obstacles that are going to stand in the way. If I try and I don't attain, at least people saw me trying. They didn't see me surrender and they didn't see me not believe. I believe and I know MONAT is on the way to $1 billion. For many it's just a dream. For me it's a challenge, and as a leader, I don't leave anything halfway. I always finish what I start.

CHAPTER 16

LEAVING A LEGACY

"WE'RE GOING to take your heart out," I remember the doctor telling me after I asked him to explain the procedure. I'll never forget those seven words or the explanation that came after as I lay in the hospital bed at the Baptist Hospital of Miami, my body connected by wires to the nearby machines. "We're going to put your heart into an incubator, and your blood circulation will continue through a machine."

"Wow," I said. "You're going to take my heart out of my body?"

"We're going to keep it active," he said. "Afterward, when we put your heart back in, we're going to give you an electric power current to activate it again."

"What if this doesn't work?" I asked.

The doctor laughed.

"No, that works," he said. "It normally works."

Two days earlier I had been driving on the highway in Miami to MONAT's office when I felt a suffocating twinge in my chest and was overcome by a sudden dizziness. The night before I felt discomfort after returning from the gym, but I assumed I had merely tweaked something. As I continued driving, I realized it was more than just a pulled muscle. When I pulled into the parking lot, I went to the urgent care conveniently located on the first floor of our office building. The staff performed an electrocardiogram, but when they couldn't get a good reading, they advised me to go to the nearby hospital. I called Leudin. "Let's meet at the hospital," I said. "I think I have something in my heart that isn't right." When I reached the hospital, my pulse registered fine and the electrocardiogram still didn't show any reason to be alarmed. The doctor said I was cleared to go back home and rest. "What I'm feeling isn't normal," I told him. "Let's do more tests." He agreed to do blood work, and when the results came in the enzymes showed that I was suffering a heart attack. There must have been a few angels taking care of me because if it hadn't been for that test, the consequences later could have been much different.

The doctors weren't sure how I had driven to the hospital, but the diagnosis was clear. I had an 80 percent obstruction in two of my arteries. The doctors told me

LEAVING A LEGACY

the situation was dangerous and that I urgently needed surgery. I didn't believe the doctors at first and wasn't ready for something so serious, but there wasn't much time to think about it. Doctors scheduled a procedure and laid out two likely outcomes: They would go in with a camera, look around at the blockage in my arteries, and, if everything went smoothly, they'd be done within forty-five minutes. Or, if needed, they'd put in coronary stents and the procedure might last three hours. I went to the operating room and my family went to the waiting room. As I lay on the operating table, still conscious, the doctor stopped. "We have to do an open heart surgery," he said. I'll never forget it. Tears rolled down my face. "Doctor, are you sure?" I asked. "Yes," he said. "This definitely is not for a stent." They wheeled me back to my hospital room and called in my family. It had been only forty minutes so when my children walked into the room, they were excited and relieved. I stared up at the ceiling, avoiding eye contact. They knew something wasn't right. "What's going on?" they asked. I held back tears as a translator helped the doctor communicate with my family, explaining that there had been a third option they hadn't mentioned in the hope it wouldn't be necessary. But now it was — I needed open heart surgery. Everyone, including me, was in shock. I'd gone from preparing for a forty-five-minute procedure to needing six-hour open heart surgery within twenty-four hours. Ray didn't sleep that night and instead investigated everything he could about the procedure and to determine I was in the best hands. The next day he was debating with the doctors using medical terms. "Are you in the medical field?" one asked him. No, he had just read everything he could on the Internet. The truth was, I was in the best place to have the surgery, and the doctors said moving elsewhere was too risky anyway. They couldn't understand how I hadn't had a "proper" heart attack. There was no time to waste — I needed surgery.

What made the situation more tense was that my mother had died in Venezuela from heart surgery complications in 2003. Like me, she had felt bad one day and had gone to the hospital. They told us they were going to do a catheterization to go in and take a closer look, which the doctors said was a simple procedure. I remember sitting in the lobby waiting for my mother's procedure to wrap up when the doctor came out with a very serious look on his face. He explained that there was an issue with my mom's blood because it was clotting too much. There was nothing they could do but put her in intensive care to try to make the blood clotting subside and attempt the procedure again. Only the day before my mom was enjoying time with us at her home. Suddenly, a doctor was telling us she was in critical

LEAVING A LEGACY

condition. It was my turn to stay with her that night, so Leudin and I and a couple of friends, Jose Luis and Dubi, stayed at the hospital. At 7 a.m., the doctor told us my mom had passed away. Everything happened so suddenly, just like with me. I was fine two days before and then complications arose. Nobody said anything about the connection, but lying in the hospital bed I kept thinking about my mom's story.

That's when the doctors explained their roles in the procedure, and I learned that my heart would be taken out of my chest. They would break my ribs to gain access, and the plan was to take two veins from my leg and substitute them for the blocked arteries. It was June 2, 2016, in the midst of MONAT's rise, and I lay on the bed waiting to be wheeled to the operating room. Ray and Leudin were the last two people I spoke to before they wheeled me down the hall. That was one of the first times I thought about my mortality and the legacy I might leave behind.

"I'm sure that I will come out of this, but if God's will is for me not to, you are responsible to make things work as they've been working until now, for the family to be united, for us to keep on fighting and working for our dreams," I told them.

Family flew in from Venezuela, and by the time I reached my scheduled surgery, there were thirty-four supporters in the waiting room. They made signs that read "Team Luis" and sat in the waiting room for six hours while doctors performed the surgery. I will always remember these moments because they remind me how strong you have to be to withstand difficult moments and live through them. I had three tubes in my stomach to drain the blood that was left in my body after surgery. The pain was suffocating. I would ask Leudin to massage my back and would tell her, "This is going to be circumstantial. I'm going to get through this." I think it was my way of showing the people around me that the strength was always there with me.

These memories always make me feel powerful and strong in difficult times in my life because when I'm going through hard times, I look back at when I was in that situation and say, "Wow, what I am going through now isn't anything compared to that." In the worst circumstances, you have to stand firm. In the worst circumstances, you have to show your best, because when we face harsh situations, no matter how difficult it is, we can make it. We can keep on going.

Two days after surgery, I got out of my bed and sat in the chair in my hospital room for the first time. I was in so much pain. "I will get out of this," I told my family. Thanks to God and thanks to the luck of life, I came back. I still had more to give.

LEAVING A LEGACY

LESSONS FOR MY CHILDREN

One of the most extraordinary times I can remember was when I moved up the ranks with Tupperware in 1985. Not because of the rank but because it was my first experience with success and allowed me to achieve financial independence. For the first time in my life, I didn't depend on the support of my parents. I depended on the income that I got through my own work.

Together with Ray, his mom and I moved out of my parents' house and into a home we rented just down the street. It was a very small house, but for me it was a palace. For the first time, my household depended on me. For as long as I could remember, up until that point my "why" was Ray. I was determined to break out of financial mediocrity and chart a new course for my family, and it made me happy to know that at last my son could have a room to sleep in. We financed furniture on credit from a local shop to fill the house and make it our home. It was at that moment I was able to identify with much more precision the value that direct sales could have in store for me. In the long term, when you have these kinds of spiritual rewards, they make you feel even more motivated. They inspire you to do more. They help you break the barriers with much more forcefulness. Having my son was one of the biggest strengths that I had in order to be able to overcome any challenge that would appear. I started organizing meetings every Thursday in my house with my sales leaders, talking about the business, the product, and, of course, sales strategies. One of the things that has always helped me is showing people what they can achieve by telling them about my own experience. I invited my team over to see with their eyes the success that I was reaching in my business and in my career.

Success didn't come easy. We couldn't stay home with Ray, so many times we left him at his grandmother's house while we drove around Venezuela to grow the Tupperware business. Family and friends criticized us a lot for doing that, but my reply was always firm. "I'm going to sacrifice being present with my son today, so in the future, my hard work can provide a better life for him." Today, I see four of my children empowered to thrive with the legacy that I created after so many years of effort. I always remind them that to be where we are now, we had to work a lot. We achieved success. But all my children know that it was due to a lot of work and many sacrifices along the way. Javier was born in 1989 and Lu in 1991, which made three children at that point. Through all those years I worked incessantly so that we could live a better life. I worked hard from Monday to Monday, driving day and night to build the business. It wasn't long before we emerged in an economical way.

LEAVING A LEGACY

But then I lost focus on what got me there and was sent to rock bottom. By then, I was married to Leudin, and we had our first child together, Luisana, and my "why" was once again creating a better life for my family. For as long as I can remember, my biggest "why" in life has been my family. When I decided to leave Tupperware and eventually start my own company, my dream was always to build something with my children. Today, Ray, Javier, and Lu are all integral parts of MONAT. Someday, if it's on their path and in their hearts, maybe Luisana and my daughter Nicole will be part of the family business too.

People ask our family, "What is the secret?" or "How do you all get along so well?" We always say, "There is no formula." I think the truth is that my children have great mothers, and together we have raised great children with the right values at heart, which for me is the foundation of my family. Our personalities balance one another out. It's not perfect. Saying that it has always been easy isn't true. It has not been easy. I've had intense arguments with Ray and very hard face-offs with Lu, but in the long term, we've understood each other and understood that alignment helps us keep harmony. (I leave Javier out because he is the harmony in the family. He's always looking for happiness for everyone.) Our family goes through a lot of challenges just like any other family, but we are committed to our relationship. Every human being who considers himself or herself a leader must be empathic and know when to insist and when it's better to leave space. Listening and paying attention to nonverbal language is imperative to being a more empathetic person. Sometimes it's important to put yourself in the place of the other person. That is an important lesson in direct selling, which is a person-to-person business, but it is applicable in all facets of life. It turns out that humility is not only an appreciable virtue but also a leadership skill that facilitates the well-being of the members of your organization. Humility means having your feet firmly on the ground and being able to recognize with the utmost objectivity your capabilities and vulnerabilities. It's never a bad thing for your team to know that you also make mistakes, that in many cases you have been afraid, that you have failed many times, and that you are human like everyone else. Humility fosters greater commitment, performance, and satisfaction as well as confidence.

I've always said it's important to be a leader by conviction, but I think in some cases it needs to be by imposition. When a leader has conviction, they reassure their people by being strong and confident and trusting their instincts. This allows people to be at ease and feel comfortable knowing they are moving along the right path. The greatest disagreements and biggest fights I've had with Lu were when she was choosing a career

LEAVING A LEGACY

path. She carried it in her blood that she wanted to be an artist, and more than once we fought in the office. I used to tell her that opening those doors was really difficult in that industry and that all the doors were open for her to develop her abilities here, in our industry, in our company. It was a gigantic battle to show her what I felt she was capable of, and I'm happy to see her now succeeding, developing her career, and investing in her dreams. Ray and Javier are more "business people," and I think Lu was afraid that she didn't fit that mold. But I saw abilities in her. I knew that we could empower her at MONAT and dared to give her responsibilities. I talked to Ray and told him we were going to put Lu in charge of the Recognition Department, which is in charge of all the rewards and the recognition program for the entire company. That gave me great satisfaction; many of her ideas have helped us get where we are today. She has done magic. And with time, I've continued to push her to explode her talent in the company. I've even taught her company finances and profit and loss statements.

In a world where almost everything is invented, leaders take on an unprecedented battle to find other leaders, people who can help cultivate new and novel ideas, who have desire and hunger and who bring a touch of ingenuity to an organization. Always remember that you are not God — we all need a team to achieve our goals. You must build and develop a team that follows and pursues your ideals, and even if at first they do not do things how you would, it's your job as a leader and teacher to show them the correct way to the goal. We must understand that to achieve success in direct sales — or in any business — you must train people, and they must be willing to step out of their comfort zone with great adaptability. Difficulties arise constantly in life and in business, so it's important to look for people who aren't afraid of adversity and know how to overcome it with creativity, emerging stronger and more resilient.

I say this to my children a lot, especially to Ray: "Train, motivate, and empower." If you don't empower your people, you're going to be a slave to your job. When you empower people, when you delegate, and when you give them the opportunity to develop themselves, you will be a leader tomorrow.

The last of John C. Maxwell's Laws of Leadership is the Law of Legacy, which begins, "What do you want people to say at your funeral? That may seem like an odd question. But it may be the most important thing you can ask yourself as a leader." It ends, "Our ability as leaders will not be measured by the buildings we built, the institutions we established, or what our team accomplished during our tenure. You and I will be judged by how well the people we invested in carried on after we are gone.

LEAVING A LEGACY

As baseball great Jackie Robinson observed, 'A life isn't significant except for its impact on other lives.'"

I wonder, *What would people say about me?*

Lying in the hospital bed with tubes in my stomach changed my life in many ways. It made me more sensitive to everything and opened my eyes to cherishing life and valuing my family. Something I learned from that experience that I say in almost all of my speeches is that every day I go out into the world in search of who I can motivate, who I can inspire, and who I can help to improve their situation. That way I give back to God all the blessings and all the opportunities that he's given me and continues giving me. When I'm surrounded by a group of people, I tell myself that if only one person leaves motivated and inspired to thrive in their life by the way I talk to them, by the way I try to inspire and motivate them, I already feel rewarded and blessed. So why do I do it? Because I will never stop feeling gratitude constantly for the blessings that God has given me. Those experiences have helped me to live with more gratitude. It's my way of saying to God that I'm thankful he took me out of those difficult situations. I was always grateful and appreciative before, but today it's something that I feel I have to do constantly as part of my routine to feel that I'm doing things correctly in the eyes of God.

I told my children that when I die, they're going to

continue with MONAT because they know what needs to be done. They know that the company isn't about them, or me, but about the team. I understood a long time ago from my love for sports that games are won in the locker room. That is, having the right attitude and predisposition to finish with success is a matter of great motivation, which is essential for the achievement of your goals.

I could have been the main character in all of this, and that could have made me feel like Superman. But I knew I couldn't have done this by myself. After my heart attack, it was easier to understand that tomorrow isn't promised to anyone. What would have happened if I had driven home that day? What if I had been the time that doctor's explanation didn't work? I thought to myself, *If I want this company to transcend time, it cannot depend on me. If I want this to transcend time, I want my children to understand that it cannot depend on them.* We must teach people, empower them, and create the leaders of tomorrow.

CHAPTER 17

BETTER NEVER STOPS

"SON, I'M DYING," I told Ray.

It was around midnight in late July 2020, and I had mustered just enough energy to call Ray from my makeshift hospital room, where I laid on the bed inside a cubicle in the COVID-19 ward. "I can't breathe," I said. "I'm very weak." Ray had already spoken to my doctor so he knew how serious the situation was. He reassured me anyway. "Dad, you're not going to die," he told me. That was the worst night of my life because I truly was dying. My blood oxygen readings were at dire levels. Ray, Javier, and Lu were preparing to donate blood plasma, hoping that it might be the antidote that could turn my COVID-19 battle around.

When COVID-19 first began four months earlier, Leudin and I boarded our yacht in the port of Miami and went to sea for forty days to protect ourselves.

REBEL LEADERSHIP

Ironically, I was living my longtime dream of managing my business from my boat. And it worked! Through empowerment and delegation set in motion in the years before, I was able to sit at the computer and help operate MONAT. In fact, in 2020, MONAT grew 300 percent. After nearly a month and a half on the water, we decided to return to land and isolate at home. For a while, we avoided COVID. But when Leudin's niece visited one day, Leudin got infected. She had a fever and some discomfort but recovered. Then it hit me. First came the fever, then the discomfort. For about six days, I moved around our home in pain. After nearly a week, I woke up in the middle of the night and turned to Leudin. "Call 9-1-1," I said. "I'm suffocating." Everything escalated after I arrived at the hospital. Two days later, I couldn't breathe.

The day after I called Ray, my doctor came to my bed. "You're in serious condition," he said. I reached out and held his hand. "Doctor, you need to get me out of here," I said. "I have many things I have to do not only for my family, but I have a company with a lot of people that are counting on me. I don't want to die."

I could barely talk. "I'm going to get through this," I told the doctor. "You're going to help me, and you and I are going to be good friends."

That day the doctors started injecting plasma. I

thought it was my salvation because the doctor said that with plasma I should recover. But thirty minutes later, I started having an allergic reaction across my entire body and they had to stop the procedure and remove it. The one hope I had to recover disappeared in an instant. At that moment, I decided to let my fate be in the hands of God and my faith in him. I called Leudin and then Ray again to share the news. "Son," I said, "it didn't work." I was worried and alone. The hospital was closed off to visitors. All I had around me was a room filled with cubicles for COVID patients.

The next day, something incredible happened: I improved. And the next day, I was discharged from the intensive care unit and moved to a regular hospital room, where I started to recover my oxygen levels. I spent eighteen days between intermediate care and intensive care, alone and isolated from the world, not knowing if I would leave the hospital alive, without the possibility of saying goodbye to my loved ones or sharing a last dinner and a glass of wine with my family. But in the midst of that picture of horror and crisis, I had the strength to take refuge in God, who gave me the strength to fight against the disease, to face it, overcome it, and defeat it. There were many things that went through my tormented head in those moments. In those eighteen days, I thought about all my dreams and unfinished goals.

REBEL LEADERSHIP

If I'm being honest, I don't go to church. I could tell you that I do, but it has never been a regular part of my life. I don't read the Bible regularly, but I have copies everywhere. There is one in my bedroom, another in the hallway outside my home office, and another downstairs. I read a few verses, but most of what I learn from the Bible I hear from my brothers and sisters, who interpret it for me. I don't read the Bible very often, but I try to live the Bible every day. Every morning — especially since I got out of the hospital — I start praying. I always thank God for his blessings. I pray for every person who is going through difficult situations. I pray for my family, my children, my siblings, and my friends. I pray for a better world for everyone. But after my prayer every day, I ask God to give me the light to have the words and the correct behaviors to motivate at least one person every day. I always try to inspire the people who I meet during the day. I feel the need to take action every day. I live by what I think God wants us to do, which is to be a good person and help other people. I know many people who read and understand the Bible but don't comply with what the Bible teaches. I understand that in the Bible, there is a concept of how to live right and do the right things. Be fair. Give thanks. Don't hate. Don't be envious. Don't hold grudges. I try to practice those lessons every day, and I say this firmly: I believe in the Word, I believe in my God, and I believe what the Bible teaches. But I also believe that action is more powerful than words, and people who talk a lot sometimes do little.

Since I started practicing this lesson, it has become a mantra in MONAT. I preach that for you to be successful, you have to make your people successful. You have to give yourself to your people for you to be able to reach your own goals. In MONAT and in the direct sales business, a selfish person doesn't succeed. The one who doesn't work for others will fail in the business. It happens a lot. Some people go into direct sales searching for money, but when they start practicing this concept of giving themselves to people and helping others reach their goals, over time, money falls to second place because they get more satisfaction from helping and supporting people than success and money. Give yourself to others, and what comes back in return will be greater.

When I was given a new lease on life a second time, I promised to search for the doctor, Pedro Sevilla, and I followed him until he accepted my offer to experience my yacht. "Come spend the weekend," I told him. "We've worked a lot," he finally admitted. "I would like for my whole team to spend a nice weekend." So on a Friday he arrived with his team of six doctors. Before they set sail into the sea off the shore of Miami, I told him, "I want to thank you for giving me my life back."

THE LADDER OF SUCCESS

When I decided to start my own business in 2001, I had nothing but a dream and a team of people who believed in the dream. During those days, someone told me something that became our mantra:

How are you doing? Good. How are you feeling? Very good. How is your situation? Better and better and better.

How are you financially? My pockets are empty. I have no money. I'm looking for my chance.

I knew that in order to have money in my bank account, first I needed to have a positive attitude and mindset. Those were the first steps toward success. The money would come later.

Success is not exclusive to anyone; it is for those who want to be the protagonists of their lives and stories, who find their True North and chase it, and who take risks without fear of failure. When things get complicated, successful people go out and act with determination, creativity, ingenuity, and with a clear purpose that with passion they will be able to reach their goal. Adversity leads many to complain, but I understood long ago that complaining doesn't bring me one inch closer to my goal. It makes no sense to waste valuable time, which could be dedicated to action that will move me closer to the finish line. There are certain principles that we can never

BETTER NEVER STOPS

put aside; they must be untouchable in your day-to-day life. Perseverance and passion must be your flags and they can never be at half-mast. You must stay ambitious; to be successful, you need motivation and responsibility, but above all you have to trust in yourself to be able to reach your goals.

To avoid failure and achieve our goals, we must be honest with ourselves, accept our surroundings, and have the courage to accept failure and lack of action instead of making excuses. In hard times, many leaders and businesspeople blame their failures on circumstances. Confidence is fundamental for entrepreneurs because it drives us to never give up and trust in our ability to solve problems and failures and move forward with our heads held high, telling us that we climbed and surpassed one more step on our ladder to success. Never neglect your confidence. It represents your individual achievements, your victories, and your passage to the next level.

I would like to illustrate my ladder to success so that you can better understand how my life experience helped me reach my goals.

DREAMS: Dreaming doesn't cost anything so what's stopping you? Dreaming is about having vision and never settling. The dreams you want to reach have to be updated regularly because when you settle for less and limit your dreams, you can surrender too easily. Some people don't chase their dreams because they are afraid they might fail. I'm more afraid of not trying. What is your dream? Do you truly believe in it? As I always say, don't let anyone steal your dream.

PASSION: Without passion it is almost impossible to achieve your dreams. When you have a passion, a True North, you're able to break through limitations. Everyone has a passion, something that sparks a fire, or something that makes him or her emotional. What is yours? Have you found it yet? Money and recognition should never be your "why." You have to be in love with what you're doing. You have to feel passionate and have a bigger purpose. That's the secret of overcoming obstacles, failures, and rejection.

HUNGER: To continue having success, you must never lose your hunger. After you succeed initially, it's important not to settle. Instead, you should chase the next milestone or look forward to the next movie in your head. Success comes from dreaming big, sacrificing what you have today for opportunity tomorrow, and making a commitment to intentional growth. Don't stop growing. Don't become complacent. Stay hungry. It's worth repeating one more time: If your hunger dies, your passion dies.

BETTER NEVER STOPS

If your passion dies, your focus dies. If your focus dies, everything will be dead.

HARD WORK: You cannot live a relaxed life and have big things. That does not exist. It's impossible to chase your dream without sacrifice. Sometimes you have to give up something good for the opportunity of something better. What are you willing to do to chase your dreams? Having talent isn't enough. That's why a less talented person who is willing to do everything it takes to pursue their passion and reach their dreams often surpasses a talented person who doesn't work hard.

PERSEVERANCE: I'll say it again: if you want to have success in life, you have to do things you like and things you don't like. It's up to you to break through those obstacles that put limits on you to do whatever it is you don't like. Success must be accompanied by sacrifice, and sometimes that means doing those things you really don't want to do. Life is made of attempts and failures, and only adventurers achieve big things.

DISCIPLINE: Discipline is the key to making everything happen. You might be capable, but without discipline, you won't reach the finish line. You might be knowledgeable, but if you don't have discipline, you're not going to make it. You have to be intentional about your daily habits, and you can't allow people or temptations to throw you off the path to your dreams. Many dreams are derailed, or worse, ruined, because someone wanders off the path and loses focus. Finish what you start.

SUCCESS: Success belongs to those who are willing to fight and climb the ladder to achieve it. The problem many people face is they think success is a destination. Success doesn't come after crossing a proverbial finish line. It comes along the journey to that dream. Respect success, respect power, and respect money. Because when you don't respect these three things, what took you to the top can also make you hit rock bottom. Some people let success make them complacent. You have to learn to learn. Until you reach your deathbed, you should keep on learning.

Charting a path toward your True North and chasing your dreams isn't just about learning; it's not just about listening to successful people, and it's not just about going somewhere to get motivated. It's also about making your goals part of your daily life. It's common for people to listen, to see, and to be motivated but not apply it, go forth, and live it. When I get out of that world that motivated me and return to real life, when I start living

BETTER NEVER STOPS

difficult moments, if I don't stay focused, I fall immediately. You have to live it. You have to say, "This is part of my life, part of what I believe in, and nobody will disrupt the vision that I have."

There are going to be challenges. There are going to be failures. Throughout your life, you will go through different types of situations. On the professional side, you will have difficulties, conflicts, challenges, and failures. On a personal level, there will also be many challenges and failures. I was ruined and went bankrupt. There are so many situations in which I had to fight to recover. I've gone through my share of medical issues too. I've broken both of my ankles, I had three surgeries on my throat as a child, and I almost died twice. What I learned on my personal ladder of success is that you have to face these challenges with a positive attitude. You have to see life in a positive light and understand that sacrifice and failure are a part of the process to reach what you want to achieve. If you don't learn to live with that, you will probably lose your spirit. If you don't learn how to live life, you will not be able to reach half of what is in store for you. I repeat: Do you believe in you? Every day lived is an invaluable experience if you know how to get ahead of the difficult times and challenges that you have in front of you on your journey.

I've failed many times in my life, but I have also

achieved many successes. Reaching the top of the ladder of success is not permanent. You will take steps back, and every new dream requires another ladder. I will keep fighting for my dream until MONAT reaches $2 billion. I promised myself that I wouldn't stop motivating my children because I know that one day the legacy will be theirs.

    I remember the day I turned to Marjorie at L'eudine as the business began to crumble. That day, I shared my dream with her: "One day we're going to be in Miami. One day we're going to have a big business. We will be so successful that I will be with Leudin on a big yacht, and I'm going to be there with my computer watching over the results of the company with a big cigar."

I did it. All of it came true. The company. The yacht.

Now, all I need is a cigar.

If God is with us, no one can be against us.

ACKNOWLEDGMENTS

I HAVE to confess, having an idea and turning it into a book is harder than I thought it was going to be. This process almost felt like a therapy session, a long one, and I was not alone. I wrote this book with an incredible group of people I feel so grateful to call family and chosen family.

I especially want to thank my wife, my pillar, my best friend, the one I built the most important part of my story with. Leudin, you are the love of my life, and if there is one thing I give thanks for every day, that's you.

I'm eternally grateful to my family. My children, Ray, Javi, Lu, Luisana, and Nicole, you all make my life what it is, and you all love me unconditionally even in my darkest moments. I have no idea where I'd be if I hadn't had all of you as my "why."

I want to thank important individuals who helped make this book happen. I will be forever grateful to Don Yeager; Katty Corobo; Marjorie Muñoz; Dubi Lugo;

ACKNOWLEDGMENTS

Jose Luis Piña; Alex Juarez; Veronica Rodriguez; my daughter-in-law, Carolina Marquez Urdaneta; my sister Yixa Urdaneta and her husband, David Julio Briceño; Mark Cole; John C. Maxwell and the whole Maxwell Leadership team; and the Forefront Books team.

I have to add that none of this would have been possible without my daughter Lu. You always told me that one day we were going to write a book with my story and my lessons, and even though I didn't fully believe you then, a few years later . . . here we are, publishing a story that became the dream of both of us.

Special thanks to my leaders of LEUDINE VENEZUELA: you all helped me when I was taking my first steps in the entrepreneurial world. Thanks to my experience with you, I learned how to make my big dreams a reality.

To everyone at the MONAT FAMILY: you all make me better, a better human, a better businessman, a better DREAMER. Thank you to all in our corporate staff and our field members for letting me lead our company with my heart; thank you for understanding my passion and embracing my "rebel style." Thank you to my son Ray for letting me be your partner in this incredible adventure and so many others. Thank you for being my best friend and the best business partner.

Most of all, I want to thank GOD, because as I always say: if God is with me, no one and nothing can be against me.

NOTES

1. John C. Maxwell, "Your Life Can Be a Great Story," *John C. Maxwell* (blog), October 20, 2015, https://www.john-maxwell.com/blog/your-life-can-be-a-great-story/

2. Angela Duckworth, speech.

3. John C. Maxwell, *The Success Journey* (Nashville: Thomas Nelson, 1997).

4. John C. Maxwell, *The 21 Irrefutable Laws of Leadership* (New York: HarperCollins Leadership, 2007).

5. Maxwell, *The 21 Irrefutable Laws of Leadership.*

6. Maxwell, *The 21 Irrefutable Laws of Leadership.*